Bertha J. Naterop

Dear Sirs

English and American
Business Correspondence

sabe
Verlagsinstitut für Lehrmittel, Zürich

DEAR SIRS
verfasst von Bertha J. Naterop
unter Mitarbeit von Bernhard Uttley BA (Computer-Kapitel)

Warum 'Dear Sirs' und nicht 'Dear Madam'
"Dear Sirs" bzw. "Gentlemen" ist im angelsächsichen Sprachraum nach wie vor die übliche Anrede in einem Schreiben an einen unbekannten Empfänger.
Diese Form hat nichts Diskriminierendes an sich und kann im deutschen Sprachraum durchaus mit «Sehr geehrte Dame/Sehr geehrter Herr» übersetzt werden.

Copyright © 1985 by sabe, Verlagsinstitut für Lehrmittel, Zürich
ISBN 3-252-03203-1
ausserdem erhältlich:
– Schlüssel ("Key to Exercises and Translations") ISBN 3-252-03204-X
– Lehrerhandbuch ISBN 3-252-03205-8

Die Autorin

Diplome der Faculty of Teachers in Commerce (Great Britain) für Englisch und Handelsfächer

Langjähriger Erwachsenenunterricht an Londoner und Zürcher Handelsschulen. Dozentin an der Volkshochschule Zürich

Experte für Englisch an KV-Lehrabschlussprüfungen, an der eidgenössischen Diplomprüfung für Kaufleute K+A sowie an den eidgenössischen Prüfungen für Direktionsassistenten. Delegierte des schweizerischen Volkshochschul-Verbandes für das internationale Zertifikat 'English for Business'

Autorin mehrerer Bücher über englische und amerikanische Handelskorrespondenz

Contents

		Page
1	The need for writing in business – confirmations and goodwill letters	7
2	Letters and envelopes: American and British Style	15
3	Appointments and meetings	22
4	Inquiries	29
5	Quotations	37
6	Offers and firm offers	47
7	Orders	55
8	Status inquiries and references	61
9	Office automation (I): the word processor	73
	Office automation (II): the computer	77
10	The warehouse	84
11	Invoices, statements and cheques	91
12	Reminders and part payments	97
13	Processing orders	105
14	Packing	113
15	Transport	119
16	Insurance	125
17	Complaints	133
18	Dealing with complaints	141
19	Marketing and distribution	147
20	Sales promotion and advertising	155
21	Banking and payments	161
22	Applications	169
23	Remarks on Grammar & Style:	
	A. How to bring good style into letter writing	177
	B. Division of words, display of a letter text	179
	C. Punctuation	180
	D. How to write numbers	182
	E. Passive	184
	F. Simple and continuous tenses	186
	G. Past, Pluperfect, Perfect	187
	H. Some prepositions in use	189
Appendix: Abbreviations and Signs		196
Word Lists		200
Wörterverzeichnis		208

1 The need for writing in business – confirmations and goodwill letters

In the old days most business transactions were simple, and there was little need for written records. There are, however, a number of historical documents that show lists and signatures for goods bartered. When the wool trade flourished between England and Continental Europe especially, traders and shippers had to produce bills of lading and declarations. At present there are still some forms of commerce where no written communication is required: cattle traders settle their deals with a handshake, shares and bonds are bought and sold by a phone call. But in most cases some form of written record is needed by the seller and by the buyer, for instance, a signed order and a cash receipt.
Nowadays business is very complex. So many types of goods and services are offered at home and abroad, and supplied in so many ways, usually on credit, that correspondence and accounts are essential.
Here are some forms of written communication:

- letters, telex, telegrams
- memoranda (including message slips)
- reports
- summaries and statistics
- minutes.

Of all forms of writing, the letter is the one most frequently used. A personal letter can be seen as a piece of conversation by post. A business letter is more than that. It is often a precise statement of agreements reached by the correspondents. As it is dated and signed it is legally binding, and serves as a record for both parties. Letters are very good too for public relations – making friends in a way. It is easier to approach a person through a letter than by means of a meeting. Then letters are used to introduce new products: direct mail advertising. A letter accompanying an enclosure (a catalogue, for example), can draw the reader's attention to certain features that are advantageous.
In a simple form a letter delivers a message in a clear and accurate way, ensuring that there are no misunderstandings or omissions, as may be the case during talks and phone conversations. That is why correspondence is written too to confirm verbal arrangements made. As a telex message is not legally binding either, a confirmation by letter is necessary when important matters are involved.

record	Unterlage, Aufzeichnung
signature	Unterschrift
goods	Güter, Waren
barter, to	austauschen
trade	Handel
flourish, to	blühen
shipper	Spediteur, Verschiffer
bill of lading	Frachtbrief, Konnossement
declaration	(Zoll)Erklärung
commerce	Handelsverkehr

cattle	Vieh
settle a deal, to	Geschäft abschliessen
share	Aktie
bond	Obligation
sign, to	unterschreiben
order	Bestellung
cash receipt	Quittung
offer, to	anbieten
supply, to	bereitstellen, beschaffen
account	Rechnung, Konto
message slip	Mitteilungszettel, Memo
report	Bericht
summary	Zusammenfassung
minutes	Notizen, Protokoll
statement	Aussage
reach an agreement, to	Übereinkunft erlangen
legally binding	rechtlich bindend
accompany, to	begleiten
enclosure	Beilage
feature	Merkmal, (Gesichts)Punkt
deliver, to	liefern
message	Mitteilung, Botschaft
omission	Unterlassung, Versäumnis
case	Fall
confirm, to	bestätigen
verbal	mündlich
arrangement	Abmachung
not ... either	auch nicht
confirmation	Bestätigung

Vocabulary exercise

Choose the correct words from the list.
1 After a phone conversation on an important ____ it is ____ to send a written ____.
2 A letter provides a ____ of the arrangements made and is ____ binding.
3 In former times there was less need for written ____ as business ____ were simple.
4 A letter can draw the reader's ____ to certain ____ that are ____.
5 A letter is one of the most ____ used forms of written ____.
6 Also a letter ____ a ____ clearly and ____.
7 A phone ____ may cause some ____ or ____.
8 When the wool trade ____ traders and shippers had to produce ____ and ____.

accurately
advantageous
attention
bills of lading
communication
confirmation
conversation
declarations
delivers
essential
features
flourished
frequently
legally
matter
message
misunderstandings
omissions
records
statement
transactions

THE UNDERSMITH CO (EUROPE) AG

12 Gotthardstrasse
6300 Zug, Switzerland

Mr S Burton
Hardcastle & Co Ltd
14 rue de la Cité
1204 Genève

7 November 19..

Dear Mr Burton

Thank you for phoning us this morning to let us know about the defective printer you received from us. We confirm the assurance we gave you verbally and we have asked Mr John Mason, of our service department, to get in touch with you today. If you have not heard from him by the time you receive this letter, would you please contact him at telephone number 022-366868.

Although our works in Cleveland have a stringent product control system, it may occasionally happen that a part or a machine is damaged in transit. Your choice of an UNDERSMITH office machine gives you a certainty, however, that you can rely on our products and our after-sales service.

Yours sincerely

THE UNDERSMITH CO AG
Service Department

cc: Undersmith London

Exoil Trading Company plc
180 Eastcheap, London EC4 G121

Deep Sea Oil Corporation
Alesund, Norway   21 January 19..

Dear Sirs

We have pleasure in confirming the telex we sent you today reading:

DEEPOIL NORGE 19..1.21
CFM ORDER FOURTEEN HUNDRED BARRELS CRUDE SU 19 GRADE AT SPOT PRICE $32 IF SUPPLIED TO ROTTERDAM BY TWENTY FEBRUARY 19.. LATER DELIVERY NOT ACCEPTED EXOIL LONDON.

As stated, we confirm ordering a quantity of 1400 barrels of crude oil SU 19 grade at the price agreed of $32.00 per barrel, but only if these are received at our company's docks in Rotterdam no later than 20 February 19.. If we are not in possession of the cargo by that date, it cannot be accepted.

We look forward to receiving your bills of lading, commercial invoice and other relevant documents soon.

                                           Yours faithfully

                                           Chief Buyer
                                           Exoil Trading Company

First National Bank Inc.
43 Commercial Road
Albington, Illinois 51032

```
Mr. Cyrus P. Thresher
1182 Fourteenth Avenue
Albington, Ill. 51032



April 17, 19..



Dear Mr. Thresher:

You've just come to Albington. Welcome.

Moving away from your former home town to a different area
brings surprises and changes for you and your family. In
the first week or two there's hardly time to find out the
attractions of your new environment. But soon your kids will
be settled in school, you'll get to know your neighbors, and
daily life will resume its more regular pattern.

We'd like to help you settle down and feel at ease as soon
as possible. Please come by to meet us. Our services are
here for you.

Sincerely yours



Samuel B. Dickens
Branch Manager




Enc: 'First' street map
     of Albington
```

assurance	Ver-, Zusicherung
stringent	streng
occasionally	gelegentlich
part	Teil
damage, to	beschädigen
in transit	unterwegs, auf dem Transport
rely on, to	sich verlassen auf
cfm (= confirm)	bestätigen
barrel	Fass
crude	roh, hier: Rohöl
spot price	Marktpreis
delivery	Lieferung
grade	Qualität
quantity	Menge
cargo	Ladung
invoice	Rechnung
possession	Besitz
relevant	massgebend, wichtig
area	Gebiet
environment	Umgebung
resume, to	fortsetzen
pattern	Muster, Vorlage

PLC or: plc Ltd	*public limited company* *limited*	*AG (britisch)*
Inc.	*incorporated company*	*AG (amerikanisch)*

Model sentences (confirmations and goodwill letters)

1. With reference to the telephone conversation we had yesterday, we ... .
2. Thank you for ringing me up to inform me of the new delivery dates.
3. We are pleased to confirm ... .
4. We have pleasure in confirming ... .
5. We had to phone you this morning to let you know about recent changes in price.
6. The telex message we received this morning was not quite clear. Would you please explain the second sentence in more detail.
7. In confirmation of our telex of today's date, we have to let you know that ... .
8. We phoned this morning, asking you to make a reservation at your hotel as follows.
9. As you are not a customer of our store yet, we would like to tell you about the many articles and services we can offer you.
10. The purpose of this letter is to introduce to you Ms Jean Simkins, who has recently been appointed to the post of export manager.
11. We look forward to meeting you and to regular business connections in the future.
12. In reply to your request by phone, we are pleased to enclose the leaflet you need.

Yours faithfully	Mit freundlichen Grüssen
(eher bei unpersönlichen Briefen)
Yours sincerely
or: Sincerely yours
Yours truly
or: Truly yours	Mit freundlichen Grüssen
(eher bei Briefen mit persönlicher Anrede)

Sentences for translation

1. Wir schreiben Ihnen, um die mündlichen Anweisungen zu bestätigen, die wir Ihnen heute telefonisch gegeben haben.
2. Wir danken Ihnen für Ihre telefonische Anfrage.
3. Gerne legen wir die verlangten Broschüren bei. [= Wir freuen uns ...] *
4. Es tut uns leid [zu erfahren],* dass Sie eine defekte Schreibmaschine erhalten haben.
5. Danke, dass Sie uns gestern telefonisch über die Änderung des Termins für unser Treffen informiert haben.
6. Es freut uns, das Telegramm zu bestätigen, das wir Ihnen heute morgen geschickt haben.
7. Die Absicht dieses Schreibens ist, Ihnen Informationen über unsere in Ihrem Land erhältlichen Produkte zu geben.
8. In Beantwortung Ihrer Telex-Anfrage von heute, freuen wir uns, (Ihnen) * eine Quittungskopie beizulegen.
9. Wir freuen uns, die Waren bis zum 19. März zu erhalten.
10. Es ist uns nicht möglich, die Waren zu akzeptieren, falls sie nach diesem Termin eintreffen.

* Words in [square] brackets help in the translation.
  Words in (round) brackets may be left out.

Letters for translation

Von: The Undersmith Co (Europe) AG, 12 Gotthardstrasse, 6300 Zug, Schweiz

An: Herrn Peter Spencer, Technischer Direktor, The Undersmith Co (UK) plc, 33 Watling Street, London EC1 2MK

20. Januar, 19..
Ihre Zeichen: PS/TT / Unser Zeichen: Techn. 42

Sehr geehrter Herr Spencer

Besten Dank für Ihren Brief vom 14. Januar, in dem Sie sich nach unserem neuen Service-Center für Zentraleuropa erkundigen.
Wir legen eine Broschüre bei, die unsere Dienstleistungen beschreibt. Auf Seite 6 [werden Sie finden] finden Sie eine Karte, die den genauen Standort unserer

Fabrik in Adliswil und die besten Wege vom Flughafen und vom Stadtzentrum Zürich aus angibt.

Wir hoffen, dass Sie uns hier bald besuchen können. Es würde uns freuen, Sie persönlich zu treffen und Ihnen vollständige Information über die hier verfügbaren Dienste zu geben.

Mit freundlichen Grüssen

Beilage: Broschüre

Letter writing assignments

1. Write a letter to The Undersmith Co (UK) plc, 33 Watling Street London EC1 2MK, confirming and explaining the following telex:
   URGENT USA BUSINESS CHANGED DATES FOR YOUR VISIT FROM 21 TO 28 FEBRUARY
   giving a reason for the change.

2. Schreiben Sie in Herrn Winklers Namen an die Hauptniederlassung:
   Undersmith Office Machine Company Inc.
   52 Third Avenue
   Cleveland, Ohio 44133
   der den folgenden Telex bestätigt:

   mr henry wedgewood, vice president

   will gladly come to headquarters 10 october to take part in planning. kindly book hotel room from 9–12 october. thanks.

   hans winkler, export sales manager

   Fügen Sie einen unverbindlichen Schlusssatz bei.

2 Letters and envelopes: American and British Style

Envelopes

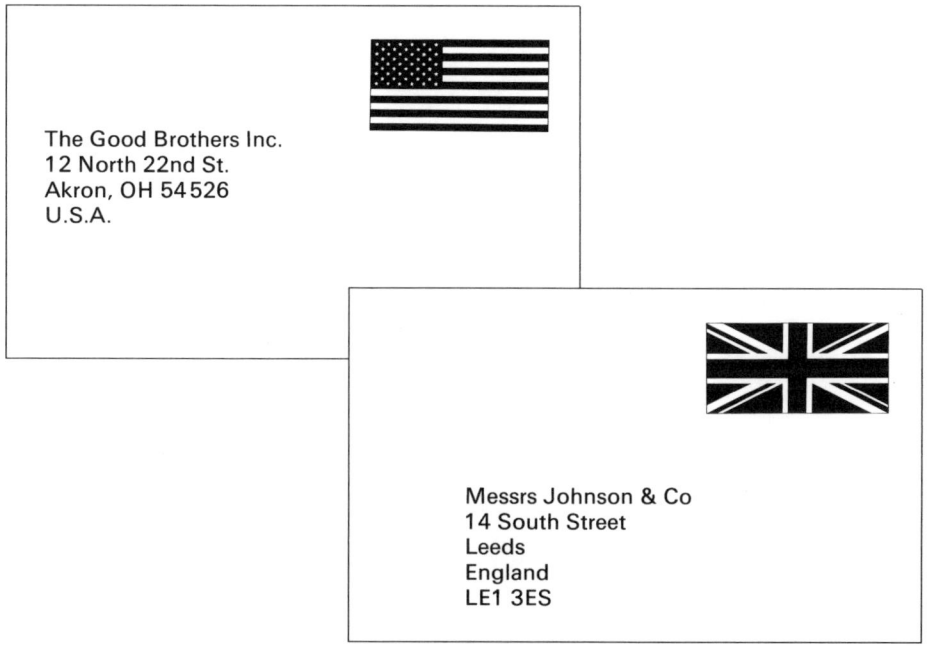

The ZIP postal code follows name of state in the U.S.A.

The British postal code follows name of town, county or country. It comes last in the address, if possible on a line by itself.

Letters

On the following pages, an example of a letter both in a typical British as well as in a widely used American form is shown.

For further information, please turn to page 18.

① # Kingston & Co
10 Field Street, Featherstone, Lancs FRE 9CE

③ Messrs Johnson & Co
14 South Street
Leeds LS1 3ES   ② 20 September 19..

④ Your ref: SL/JB
Our ref: BH/312

⑤ Dear Sirs

⑥ <u>Visit of your representative</u>

⑦ Thank you for your letter of 18 September, in which you ask us to let you know when it would be convenient for your representative to call on us.

Our Mr Thornton will be away for the rest of this week. May we therefore suggest Tuesday 28 September as a date for your representative's visit? Please inform us at what time he plans to call on us.

⑧ Yours faithfully
KINGSTON & CO LTD

⑨ John M Davidson
Sales Manager

⑩ Enc: company map

①   **THE STATE SUPPLIERS INC.**
419 West Street   Houston, Texas 83192

③   The Good Brothers Inc.
      12 North 22nd St.
      Akron, OH 54526

②   September 20, 19..

④   Your ref.: SL/JB
      Our ref.: BH/312

⑥   **Visit of your representative**

⑤   Gentlemen:

⑦   Thank you for your letter of September 18, in which you ask us to let you know when it would be convenient for your representative to call on us.

      Our Mr. Thornton will be away for the rest of this week. May we therefore suggest Tuesday, September 28 as a date for your representative's visit? Please inform us at what time he plans to call on us.

⑧   Very truly yours

⑨   Peter J. Brooks
      Sales Manager

⑩   Enc.: company map

	Great Britain	USA	Remarks
① Printed heading			Includes name, address, telephone number (* telegraphic address, description of business, directors' names, products)
② Date	6th November 19.. 6 November 19..	November 6, 19..	No mention of town
③ Inside address	Mr R Reader, or R Reader Esq Messrs Johnson & Co 14 South Street Leeds LS1 3ES	Mr. John R. Sands The Good Brothers Inc. 12 North 22nd St. Akron, OH 54526	American titles and initials are generally followed by a period. Messrs is plural of Mr and should be used for companies naming two or more persons.
	For the attention of Mr R Johns or Mr R Johns c/o National Bank Ltd.		Two lines below inside address
④ Reference*			Initials or number
⑤ Salutation	Dear Sirs	Gentlemen:	See next page
⑥ Subject line	After salutation	Before salutation	
⑦ Body of letter	Block form or indented	Block form	
⑧ Complimentary close	Yours faithfully	Very truly yours	First word starts with capital letter. See next page
⑨ Signature			Signed by one person only. Signed name, writer's status, * company
⑩ Enclosure*			

* May be left out.

Salutation and complimentary close

	Great Britain	**USA**
Formal or routine correspondence	Dear Sir Dear Madam Dear Sirs Mesdames (Ladies) Dear Sir or Madam	Gentlemen: Dear Madam: Dear Sir: Ladies: (Mesdames) Dear Ms. Brown (when in doubt as to the marital status)
	Yours faithfully Yours very truly	Very truly yours Sincerely yours
Correspondents know each other	Dear Mr Brown Dear Mrs Smith Dear Ms Brown	Dear Mr. Brown: Dear Miss Roberts: Dear Mrs. Smith:
	Yours truly Yours sincerely	Sincerely yours Cordially yours
Good business friends	Dear Jim Dear Mr Brown My dear Brown	Dear Jim: Dear Mr. Brown: My dear Mr. Brown:
	Yours sincerely	Cordially yours With best regards
Personal letter	Same	(My) Dear Mr. Brown Dear Jim
	With kind regards With best regards Yours sincerely	With best regards Most sincerely
Official correspondence	Sir Dear Mr Mayor	Sir: Dear Senator Fuller:
	Yours faithfully Yours very truly	Respectfully yours Very sincerely yours

Differences in English and American* spelling and usage

English	**American**	**German**
accident insurance	casualty insurance	*Unfallversicherung*
aeroplane	airplane	*Flugzeug*

* Whichever form is chosen, English or American, uniformity should be maintained throughout the letter or report.

English	American	German
aluminium	aluminum	*Aluminium*
autumn	fall	*Herbst*
bonded warehouse	customs warehouse	*Zollfreilager*
brackets	parentheses	*Klammern*
car	automobile / car	*Auto*
carriage, freight	freight	*Fracht*
carriage forward	freight forward / collect	*unfrankiert, unfranko*
cash on delivery	collect	*Nachnahme*
catalogue	catalog	*Katalog*
chartered accountant	Certified Public Accountant	*beeidigter Bücherrevisor*
cheque	check	*Scheck*
Christian name	first name	*Vorname*
cinema	movies	*Kino*
commercial traveller	traveling salesman	*Handelsreisender*
consignment note	waybill	*Frachtbrief*
counterfoil	stub	*Kontrollabschnitt*
crossed cheque	check with restrictive endorsement	*Verrechnungsscheck*
current account	checking account	*Kontokorrent*
to fill in (a form)	to fill out (a form)	*ausfüllen*
first floor	second floor	*1. Stockwerk*
flat	apartment	*Wohnung*
fortnight	two weeks	*vierzehn Tage*
full stop	period	*Punkt*
goodbye	goodby	*auf Wiedersehen*
goods train	freight train	*Güterzug*
ground floor	first floor	*Erdgeschoss*
guarantee	guaranty	*Garantie*
half an hour	a half hour	*halbe Stunde*
head office	home office	*Hauptsitz*
holiday	vacation	*Ferien*
to inquire, enquire	to inquire	*anfragen*
jewellery	jewelry	*Schmuck*
label	tag	*Etikett*
to let, lease	to rent (out), to lease (out)	*vermieten*
lift	elevator	*Aufzug*
lorry	truck	*Lastwagen*
Ltd	Inc.	*AG*
luggage	baggage	*Gepäck*
order form	order blank	*Bestellungsformular*
packet	pack	*kleines Paket*
parcel	package	*Paket*
petrol	gas (oline)	*Benzin*
to phone	to call (preferred)	*telefonieren*
post, mail	mail	*Post*
postcode	Zip code	*Postleitzahl*
railway	railroad	*Eisenbahn*
return ticket	round-trip ticket	*Rückfahrkarte*
ring up	call (up)	*telefonieren*
shareholder	stockholder	*Aktionär*
shop	store	*Laden*
shop assistant	salesman, sales girl	*Verkäufer(in)*
shorthand typist	stenographer	*Stenotypist(in)*

English	American	German
stroke (19/2)	slash	*Schrägstrich*
strongroom	vault	*(Geld-)Tresor*
surname	last name	*(Familien-)Name*
telegram	cable	*Telegramm*
testimonial	letter of recommendation	*Zeugnis*
third-party insurance	liability insurance	*Haftpflichtversicherung*
tyre	tire	*Reifen*
underground	subway	*Untergrundbahn*
million	million	*1 000 000*
thousand million	billion	*1 000 000 000*
billion	trillion	*1 000 000 000 000*
thousand billion	quadrillion	*1 000 000 000 000 000*

Words ending in -our

labour	labor	*Arbeit*
colour	color	*Farbe*
neighbour	neighbor etc.	*Nachbar*

Words ending in -re

centre	center	*Zentrum, Mitte*
metre	meter	*Meter*
theatre	theater etc.	*Theater*

Certain words ending in -ce

defence	defense	*Verteidigung*
licence	license	*Bewilligung*
vice	vise	*Schraubstock*

Certain double letters

travelled/traveller	traveled/traveler	*gereist, Reisender*
cancelled	canceled	*abgesagt*
waggon	wagon	*Güterwagen*
woollen	woolen	*wollen (aus Wolle)*

Words of French origin ending -mme

kilogramme	kilogram	*Kilogramm*
programme	program	*Programm*

3 Appointments and meetings

It belongs to the task of a personal assistant or a secretary of a manager to keep a diary or an appointment book, and to make travel arrangements and appointments. In addition there are meetings, courses and conferences in the office or elsewhere, for which preparations have to be made several weeks or months in advance.
Meetings may be informal or formal. An informal meeting can be attended by two or three people, or by numerous persons. Notes of an informal meeting may form the basis for a report or a letter, in which the most important points dealt with are documented. In cooperation with the manager or the chairman of a formal meeting, the secretary will send a notice or an invitation with the agenda listing the topics to be discussed. While the meeting is held notes should be taken for the minutes, i.e. the record of the discussions and the resolutions passed.
The people attending meetings at home or abroad often have to travel and will need hotel accommodation. The booking of flights is best handled by an airline or travel agency, and the company receiving a visitor will usually take care of accommodation locally.

appointment	Verabredung
arrangement	Vorbereitung
task	Aufgabe
diary	Tagebuch, Taschenkalender
in addition	zusätzlich
course	Kurs, Lehrgang
elsewhere	anderswo
in advance	im voraus
take notes, to	Notizen machen
attend, to	teilnehmen, beiwohnen
numerous	zahlreich
deal with, to	behandeln
chairman	Vorsitzender
notice	Mitteilung, Ankündigung
list, to	auflisten
topic	Thema, Traktandum
i.e.	d.h. (das heisst)
pass a resolution, to	Beschluss verabschieden
accommodation	Unterkunft
locally	örtlich

Vocabulary exercise

Choose the correct words from the list.
1 A secretary is expected to keep an ____ book up to date.   abroad

2 A personal assistant, too, has the ____ of making arrangements for ____ or ____ which are held out of town.
3 It is best to prepare for these several weeks ____.
4 The people who are going to ____ a meeting receive a ____ with the agenda.
5 The ____ to be discussed are listed in the agenda which is ____ with the notice.
6 During a ____ notes should be taken for the ____ that are ____ afterwards.
7 These are the ____ of discussions and ____.
8 People going to meetings ____ may have to ____ by air.
9 An ____ or travel ____ can book the ____.
10 They can also reserve ____ at a hotel.

accommodation
agency
airline
appointment
attend
conferences
courses
documented
enclosed
flights
in advance
meeting
minutes
notice
records
resolutions
task
topics
travel

Watch out with these words

Agenda	diary	agenda	*Traktandenliste*
aktuell	at present, up-to-date	actually	*tatsächlich*
bekommen	get	become	*werden*
denn	because	then	*dann (zeitlich)*
dezente Farben	quiet colours	decent	*anständig*
endlich	at last	finally	*schliesslich*
eventuell	possibly	eventually	*schliesslich*
Existenz	living, earnings	existence	*Bestehen*
gegenwärtig	at present	presently	*in nächster Zeit*
eine Kapazität	an authority	capacity	*Rauminhalt, Fassungsvermögen*
		in my capacity	*in meiner Eigenschaft*
kompetent	responsible	competent	*fähig*
Konjunktur	state of business	conjuncture	*Wendepunkt*
konsequent	consistent	consequently	*folglich, als Folge*
die Konsequenzen ziehen	draw one's conclusions	take the consequences	*die Konsequenzen tragen*
Magazin	store, warehouse	magazine	*Unterhaltungszeitschrift*
Notiz	note	notice	*bemerken*
Novelle	short story	novel	*Roman*
Occasions-	second-hand	occasion	*Gelegenheit*
Prospekt	leaflet	prospectus	*Emissionsprospekt*
prüfen	check	prove	*beweisen*
sensibel	sensitive	sensible	*vernünftig*
übernehmen	take over	overtake	*überholen*

THE UNDERSMITH CO (EUROPE) AG
12 Gotthardstrasse
6300 Zug, Switzerland

To: Sales managers at all branch offices   12 December 19..

Dear Colleagues

<u>Sales Promotion</u>

Our annual sales conference is due next month. At the suggestion of Mr Henry Wedgewood, Vice President at our Cleveland USA Headquarters, it will be devoted mainly to sales promotion and our new advertising campaign to be launched in spring.

The conference will be held at our offices in Zug from Monday, 14 January to Wednesday, 16 January 19... You are cordially invited to attend or, if you are prevented by urgent reasons from doing so, your assistant sales manager should be delegated. Our first meeting will begin at 10.30 am on 14 January, as you will see from the provisional programme attached. Accommodation is being reserved at the Hotel Rössli, Zug. Would you kindly inform me whether you will be arriving on Sunday or Monday, and on what date you plan to leave the hotel?

Your budget for the coming year has already been received, and the accounts for this year are expected in the meantime. If any alterations in the budget are planned on the basis of these figures, I should like to receive your proposals by 10 January.

I am looking forward to seeing you next month, and send you and your family my best wishes for Christmas and the New Year.

　　　　　　　　　　　　　　　　　With kind regards

　　　　　　　　　　　　　　　　　THE UNDERSMITH CO (EUROPE)
　　　　　　　　　　　　　　　　　Export Sales Director

Enc: Programme

                    The Hutton Wholesalers Ltd
                    125 King William Sreet
                    London EC4 3PJ

The Sales Manager
Master Watches S.A.
2400 Le Locle, Suisse   28th February 19..

Dear Sir or Madam

   As the chief buyer of our company, I should very much
like to meet a representative of yours when I come to the
Basle Trade Fair next week. There is a growing demand for
your newly styled watches, and we are considering the import of a certain quantity.

   Would it be convenient if I come to your stand at 2.30
on Thursday, 7th March? Perhaps you could let me know, or
suggest an alternative date.

                              Yours faithfully

                              F Winston
                              Chief Buyer

be convenient, to	gelegen sein
representative	Vertreter
annual	jährlich
be due, to	fällig sein
devote, to	widmen
launch, to	lancieren
cordial	herzlich
prevent, to	verhindern
delegate, to	delegieren
provisional	provisorisch, vorläufig
attach, to	beifügen, beiheften
meantime	Zwischenzeit
alteration	Änderung
figure	Zahl
proposal	Vorschlag
kind regards	beste Grüsse
fair	Messe
demand	Nachfrage
consider, to	in Betracht ziehen

Dates

(Written)	(In speaking, dictating)
18 September	the 18th of September
September 18	September the 18th

Model sentences (appointments and meetings)

1 Mr YZ, marketing manager, is visiting several customers in the Manchester area next month.
2 Would you please let us know which dates would suit you for his visit.
3 Could you leave a message at my hotel, letting me know what time would be convenient for me to pay you a visit?
4 As arranged by phone, we expect you at our offices at 4.30 pm on 12 September.
5 We look forward to making your acquaintance/renewing the acquaintance.
6 Our chief buyer will be engaged on the dates you plan to call on us. We suggest the afternoon of March 17 for a meeting.
7 Would you please arrange to meet Mr Cox at Heathrow Airport. His plane is due at 9.15 hours on 2 April, flight KL 347.
8 In reply to your request for hotel reservations, we are enclosing three brochures giving details of accommodation and terms.
9 Would you be so kind as to book hotel accommodation (bed and breakfast only) for the period of the conference.
10 We confirm that we have reserved the rooms requested at the Crest Hotel.
11 Thank you for letting me know of Mr Michael's planned visit in May.

Sentences for translation

1. Eine Sekretärin hält normalerweise die Agenda ihres Chefs auf dem laufenden.
2. Vorbereitungen für Treffen und Konferenzen werden einige Wochen im voraus getroffen.
3. Wir freuen uns, Ihnen die Tagesordnung zuzustellen, in der die Traktanden für Ihr Treffen mit Ms X aufgelistet sind.
4. Lassen Sie uns bitte wissen, wieviel Personen am Lehrgang teilnehmen werden und ob Sie eine Hotelunterkunft benötigen, indem Sie die beiligende Karte ausfüllen.
5. Wir haben Sie heute morgen angerufen und gebeten, in Ihrem Hotel eine Reservation vorzunehmen.
6. Jetzt kann ich Sie wissen lassen, dass die Flugbuchung, die Sie mich baten vorzunehmen, definitiv ist.
7. Können Sie mir mitteilen, wann Ihnen in den nächsten zwei Monaten ein Treffen passen würde.
8. Herr Michael freut sich darauf, Ihre Bekanntschaft zu machen.
9. Würde Ihnen nächster Donnerstag für eine Zusammenkunft passen?
10. Wären Sie so nett und würden Sie für unseren Chefeinkäufer eine Nachricht in seinem Hotel hinterlassen?

Letters for translation

1. Von: Johnson & Co Ltd, Engineering Works, 23 Upton Street, Sheffield SM5 2CF
   An: Limmat Papierfabrik AG, Limmatstrasse 425, 8005 Zürich, Schweiz
   10. Oktober 19..

   Sehr geehrte Damen und Herren

   Wir mussten Sie heute anrufen, um Ihnen mitzuteilen, dass unser Vertreter, Herr Peter Blake, der plante, Sie nächste Woche zu besuchen, leider nicht in der Lage ist zu kommen. Krankheitshalber wird er mindestens für den Rest der Woche hierbleiben müssen. Er ist jedoch nicht ernsthaft krank und hofft, später im Monat nach Zürich kommen zu können.
   Wir hoffen, dass die Verschiebung Ihnen nicht allzu grosse Unannehmlichkeiten bereitet.
   Herr Blake wird sich mit Ihnen in Verbindung setzen, sobald er seine Reise zu Ihnen geplant hat.

   Mit freundlichen Grüssen

2. Von: The Undersmith Co (UK) plc, 33 Watling Street, London EC1 2MK

   An: Herrn S. Gassmann, Technischer Direktor, The Undersmith Co (Europe) AG, Gotthardstrasse 12, 6300 Zug, Schweiz

   24. Januar 19..

   Sehr geehrter Herr Gassmann

   Besten Dank für Ihre Broschüre, die Sie mir mit Ihrem Brief vom 20. Januar 19.. zugestellt haben. Die Dienstleistungen, die Sie beschreiben, sind in der Tat mannigfaltiger als diejenigen, die wir bis anhin unseren Kunden geben konnten.
   Ja, ich würde Sie sehr gerne besuchen. Es würde mir passen, zu Ihnen während der zweiten Februarhälfte zu kommen, wenn ich von einer Geschäftsreise aus Italien zurückkehre. Bitte teilen Sie mir mit, welche Daten Ihnen für meinen Besuch passen würden.

   Mit freundlichen Grüssen

Letter writing assignments

Write a reply to the letter from the chief buyer of Hutton Wholesalers Ltd (p. 25) in which you invite Mr Winston to visit your stand on the date suggested. Your sales manager, Mr P Schmidt, already has an engagement at 2.30 but could change this or, preferably, see him at 3.30 or 4 o'clock.

4 Inquiries

A businessman writes an inquiry (also spelt *enquiry*) when he wants some information on the supply of goods. He may have seen the products at a trade fair, or have read about them in an advertisement, a trade index or a catalogue, or perhaps he has had a recommendation from someone he knows. An inquiry is sometimes made by phone, but a letter giving full details on the quantity of goods required and when, helps the supplier to make the right type of quotation. It is useful too if the prospective customer describes his business and for what purpose he needs the goods in question.

Besides asking about the prices and delivery times of the goods he needs, the customer may want leaflets, catalogues and/or samples. He must also know the terms of payment, that is if a discount can be granted for a large quantity or for payment within a certain time, and whether freight and insurance are included in the prices quoted.

inquiry/enquiry	*Anfrage*
trade index	*Branchenverzeichnis*
recommendation	*Empfehlung*
supplier	*Anbieter, Lieferant*
quotation	*Preisangabe, Notierung*
prospective	*voraussichtlich, künftig*
purpose	*Absicht, Zweck*
in question	*in Frage stehend*
delivery	*Lieferung*
leaflet	*Flugblatt, Prospekt*
sample	*Muster*
terms of payment	*Zahlungsbedingungen*
discount	*Rabatt*
grant, to	*gewähren*
freight	*Fracht*
insurance	*Versicherung*
included	*inbegriffen*
quote, to	*angeben, (Kurse) notieren*

Vocabulary exercise

Choose the correct words from the list.
1 If a businessman has had a ____ from someone he knows, he may make an ____.
2 A businessman can make a phone ____ when he wants to know about the ____ of ____.
3 It is better for him to write a letter, so that the ____ knows exactly what he ____.

call
customer
delivery
discount
freight
goods
granted

4 Two of the most ____ things a new ____ wants to know are the ____ and the ____ time.
5 It is useful if he also receives a ____ or a ____ which shows him what the product looks like.
6 The price is influenced by the ____ of payment, because there may be quite a reduction for a large ____, or when ____ is made within one or two weeks.
7 Such a ____ is also ____ when goods are ordered regularly.
8 Another thing a ____ buyer want to know is whether ____ and ____ are included in the price.

important
inquiry
insurance
leaflet
payment
price
prospective
quantity
recommendation
requires
sample
supplier
supply
terms

---

erhalten to receive: *empfangen, entgegennehmen*
to obtain: *erlangen, bekommen, verschaffen*
to acquire: *(Eigenschaften) erwerben*
to get: *bekommen*
(conversational; should be used sparingly in correspondence)

If the express letter is sent off today you will receive it tomorrow.
Where can we obtain good walking shoes?
He acquired a good knowledge of English.
Did you get the cable in time?

Woodsmann & Co
27 Strand
London W1V 7HA

```
The Undersmith Co AG
12 Gotthardstrasse
CH-6300 Zug                        14 June 19..


Dear Sirs

I have seen your advertisement in 'The Times' and would
be interested in having further details of the printers
and word processing equipment you offer.

In our office we are considering replacing our standard
typewriters by electronic machines. or word processing
equipment.

Would you please explain to us what advantages your
systems can give us. Please send us your price lists
with terms of payment and illustrated leaflets.

I hope it will be possible to make the changeover within
the next two months.


                              Yours faithfully



                              H R Wells
                              Company Secretary
```

International Traders Inc.

56 Central Street
Seattle 98122

The State Suppliers Inc.
419 West Street
Houston, Texas 77037

November 9, 19..

Supply of Deck Chairs

Gentlemen:

Your address has been given us by Messrs. James & Johnson of this city, who inform us that you are the leading manufacturers of deck chairs.

We have an inquiry from wholesalers who have a large number of branches. If you can let us have a really competitive quotation for deck chairs which you have in stock, we may be able to place large orders.

                        Very truly yours

                        International Traders Inc.
                        Chief Buyer

SNOWSPORT SHOE COMPANY
5000 Aarau, Switzerland

Walkwell Footwear Company plc
Export Department
Northampton N19 3AF
England   13 September 19..

Dear Sirs

We owe your address to Messrs Lightman Ltd of Gloucester, who have been business friends of ours for the last six years. They inform us that you are one of the leading producers of gentlemen's sports shoes in your country.

As we plan to extend our range of shoes, we request you to send us your latest catalogue or descriptive literature with a price-list. Will you please quote us your most favourable terms for the resale of these goods. If your footwear meets our requirements and your prices leave us a fair margin of profit, we can probably place considerable orders.

We await your early answer.

                                    Yours faithfully

                                    Snowsport Shoe Company

The Bird Pen Company
67 High Street
London EC5 2RM

Plastiglass Inc
1492 Columbus Avenue
New York, NY 10036
USA   25 October 19..

Dear Sirs

Will you please let us have a sample of your quality BA plastic which was shown recently at the Plastics Exhibition in London. We shall shortly require this material for the manufacture of small boxes for our ball-point pens.

If, however, you can supply a similar quality which you consider more suitable at the same price, we shall be glad to receive details by return mail.

                                       Yours faithfully
                                       THE BIRD PEN COMPANY

                                       J Jackson
                                       Packaging Department

deck chair	Liegestuhl
manufacturer	Hersteller
wholesaler	Grossist
competitive	konkurrenzfähig
stock	Lager
exhibition	Ausstellung
similar	gleichartig
suitable	passend
by return (of) mail	postwendend
owe, to	schulden
extend, to	ausweiten
range	Sortiment
request, to	ersuchen
favourable	günstig, vorteilhaft
resale	Wiederverkauf
footwear	Schuhwerk
meet the requirements	Anforderungen entsprechen

Model sentences (inquiries)

1. I wonder whether you could give me some information.
2. There is a growing demand for your product in this country, and we would like to extend our range to include these articles.
3. We should be very grateful for full details.
4. Would you be kind enough to let me know your best terms for sports shoes in the usual sizes.
5. I should very much appreciate it if you would let me have a competitive quotation.
6. Your company has been recommended to us by the Chamber of Commerce.
7. We saw your products demonstrated at the Trade Exhibition.
8. We understand that you are producers of office furniture.
9. Please send us a quotation for 2000 cases of Scotch whisky, which we shall need shortly.
10. Would you kindly quote us your best prices and terms of payment for typewriters.
11. If your prices are competitive, we can probably place regular orders.
12. Please quote your discounts for regular purchases and for large quantities.
13. We look forward to receiving your quotation with samples by return.
14. Thank you in advance for any information you can give us.

Sentences for translation

1. Wollen Sie uns bitte Ihre Preise und Zahlungsbedingungen angeben.
2. Wir möchten gerne Ihren neusten Katalog erhalten.
3. Da er ein guter Kunde ist, werden wir versuchen, ihm einen Sonderrabatt zu gewähren.
4. Wir sind an Ihren Artikeln interessiert und würden gerne ein Prospekt erhalten.

5. Die Preisliste erwähnt alle Einzelheiten über Rabatte.
6. Wir benötigen Muster von Artikeln, die nicht (all)zu teuer sind und die Sie bald liefern können.
7. Falls Ihre Bedingungen günstig sind, werden wir wahrscheinlich eine ansehnliche Bestellung vornehmen.
8. Zu diesen konkurrenzfähigen Preisen verkaufen sich unsere Artikel sehr gut.
9. Die angegebenen Preise schliessen Fracht und Versicherung mit ein.
10. Falls Sie dieselbe Art Plastik nicht an Lager haben, könnten Sie uns dann eine ähnliche, geeignete Qualität anbieten?
11. Könnten Sie mir einige Angaben über die Lieferzeit machen?

Letters for translation

1. Von: Victor A. Sims, Import Agent, Nicosia, Cyprus
   An: Morris Motors Ltd, 66 Prior Street, Oxford OX6 7BR England

   19. März 19..

   Sehr geehrte Herren

   Seit einigen Jahren verkaufen wir Ihre Morris Oxford-Autos. Jetzt wollen wir versuchen, auch Ihre anderen Modelle zu verkaufen.
   Wir würden gerne die Exportpreise und Lieferfristen der neuesten Modelle erfahren.

2. An: Messrs. E.I.du Pont de Nemours & Co, 7 South Dearborn Street, Chicago, Illinois 60643

   18. April 19..

   Wir senden Ihnen beiligend eine Probe Plastikmaterial. Wir würden gerne von Ihnen erfahren [= hören], ob Sie dieses Material liefern können und zu welchem Preis. Falls Sie diese Qualität nicht am Lager haben, bitten wir Sie, uns Proben ähnlicher Plastikmaterialien zu senden. Die Materialien müssen von sehr guter Qualität sein.
   Wollen Sie uns Ihre Preise nennen und uns mitteilen, ob Sie einen Rabatt von 5% gewähren können.

Letter writing assignments

Sie haben von der Schwedischen Handelskammer in Zürich die folgende Anschrift eines Büromöbelherstellers erhalten:
Torsson & Sons, Surbrunnsgatan 81, 113 27 Stockholm, Schweden
Schreiben Sie dieser Firma und fragen Sie nach einem Katalog, nach Zahlungsbedingungen, Wiederverkaufsrabatten und sonstigen Preisnachlässen ab gewissen Bezugsmengen. Schliessen Sie den Brief mit einem optimistischen Satz ab.

5 Quotations

In reply to an inquiry from a customer a supplier sends a quotation. This is usually written as a letter, though a printed quotation is often used too. The quotation informs the prospective buyer about the goods to be supplied, the price, delivery time and the terms of payment. It may contain a description of the articles in question and alternative products, and the writer can point out the benefits resulting from placing regular orders. Then, questions of packing, transport and insurance, which affect the price, can be included. A catalogue or a leaflet and a price-list should be enclosed, or sent under separate cover, to give the recipient full details of the articles he wants and others which the company would like to sell. Samples show even more clearly the quality and design of the goods offered. Price-lists are usually printed separately so as to incorporate recent changes.

A quotation should be seen as a sales letter. Although the type of goods wanted, the price and so on are paramount, a good letter can also contribute to winning the order. That is why a friendly and helpful approach is important, and this is the reason why a letter is preferred rather than an impersonal form.

Many inquiries call for the same information. In this case a standard letter can be written and copied in relevant cases. A more efficient system is to have quotations typed by an automatic typewriter or produced by a word processor. But where the customer has special needs, or if the supplier wants to draw his attention to favourable terms, a sales manager will write a letter individually although it is more time-consuming. Many firms, after all, spend thousands of pounds advertising to create customer interest. So when interest is shown by the inquirer, the answer should be a good sales-promoting letter.

Note: See chapter 9 for more information on office automation and word processing.

printed	*gedruckt*
contain, to	*beinhalten*
alternative	*alternativ*
benefit	*Vorteil, Nutzen*
regular	*regelmässig*
affect, to	*beeinflussen*
under separate cover	*gesondert*
recipient	*Empfänger*
design	*Formgebung, Konstruktion*
incorporate, to	*aufnehmen*
paramount	*ausschlaggebend, überragend*
contribute, to	*beitragen*
time-consuming	*zeitraubend*
create, to	*(er)schaffen, erzeugen*
inquirer	*Anfragender, Fragesteller*
promote, to	*fördern, unterstützen*

Vocabulary exercise

Choose the correct words from the list.
1. After a customer has made an inquiry, the ____ will send a ____.
2. Two important details are the ____ time and the ____ of payment.
3. The supplier can ____ a catalogue or send it under ____.
4. It is useful to have a ____ of the articles to be supplied, but ____ show exactly what the articles look like.
5. A price-____ is a separate sheet, because prices usually ____ more often than the catalogue.
6. A well-written letter can ____ towards ____ the order.
7. A quotation form is rather ____, and that is why a letter is ____.
8. When a company receives many similar ____, they can reply by ____ letter.
9. But a ____ manager should write a special letter when the ____ has special needs, even though it is more time-____.
10. Advertising is a more ____ way of attracting customers than a sales-____ letter.
11. A catalogue can give the ____ more ____ of the articles he wants.

change
consuming
contribute
customer
delivery
description
details
enclose
expensive
impersonal
inquiries
list
preferred
promoting
quotation
recipient
sales
samples
separate cover
standard
supplier
terms
winning

bis	by: not later than a certain time ... if we receive your order by 20th instant. until, till: the period an action lasts He waited until two o'clock. to: usually used with "from" Office hours are from nine to five o'clock. up to: usually used with amounts ... allow us a credit up to £ 300.
bis jetzt	so far: until present time Business has been brisk so far. as yet: until present time (with negative) No plans have been made as yet.

91 Newton Road   **JACKSON BROS.**   Buxton, Derby L528 9BW

*The Clarkson Company
15 Burberry Street
Lancaster LB2 7YZ   1 June 19..

Dear Sirs

Our range of popular artificial silks has been sent to you today
by parcel post. We trust that you will be able to make a selection
from this year's new materials, the colours of which are absolutely
fast.

We have asked our representative, Mr Bernhard Robinson, to call on
you next week, in case you wish to have further information on prices,
terms and times of delivery. Of course, he will take the liberty of
ringing you up beforehand in order to arrange a suitable time.

We trust that you will find this new line to your liking, and that
we may expect an order from you in due course.

Any order you place, be it large or small, will receive our best
attention.

                                        Yours faithfully

                                        JACKSON BROS
                                        Joan White
                                        Sales Manager

MORRIS MOTORS OXFORD
66 Prior Street
Oxford OX6 7BR

Ref: JW/ST

Mr Victor A Sims
Car Dealer
Nicosia Cyprus   23 March 19..

Dear Mr Sims

Of course we are pleased to send you prices for the 19.. Morris passenger cars which you inquired about in your letter of 20 March. You will also be interested in the attached catalogue and folders, which should be of help to you. We can promise delivery four weeks after receiving your order.

We are always glad to answer inquiries about our products. So, if you need any more information, please let us know.

                                        Yours sincerely

                                        MORRIS MOTORS OXFORD

Birmingham Tool Co Ltd
224 Snow Street
Birmingham BIR OAA, England

Messrs Asher & Co
Tel-Aviv, Israel

2 February 19..

Dear Sirs

We refer to your letter of 30 January and confirm our telegram of today reading:

PRICES REQUESTED THREE POUNDS PER DOZEN TWENTY POUNDS PER HUNDRED FOB LONDON STOP PRICE-LISTS ETC MAILED TODAY BRUMTOOLS

The special steel spanners about which you inquired are shown as item No 403/21 on the price-lists enclosed. You will find an illustration giving the sizes on page 4 of the folder which is also accompanying this letter.

We regret that it is not possible for us to quote prices cif Haifa, as all our sales are effected fob London. If you wish, our forwarding agents, Messrs Harrington Bros, 49 Upper Thames Street, London EC4N 1NK, can let you know the freight and insurance charges involved. On the other hand, your own forwarders in Israel will be in a position to calculate the cif prices.

In the case of your first order our terms are Cash with Order. On repeat orders we could grant you 30 days' credit less 5% discount, or 60 days net. As prices are rising we would advise you to order soon.

Always with pleasure at your service,

                                                    we are,
                                                  Yours faithfully
                                                  BIRMINGHAM TOOL CO LTD

                                                  A Moody
                                                  Export Department

Enc: Price-list
      Illustrated folder

Master Watches S.A.
2400 Le Locle, Suisse

F Winston Esq, Chief Buyer
The Hutton Wholesalers Ltd
125 King William Street
London EC4 3PJ   14 March 19..

Dear Mr Winston

It was a pleasure to meet you at our stand at the Basle Trade Fair last week, and I should like now to confirm the offer I made.

We can deliver the Mini-Watch Mod. 05 at a price of Sfr 324 a dozen per 6 dozen or over. The delivery time will be about one month. The Mini-Watch Mod. 07 will cost Sfr 420 a dozen and can be delivered immediately. The minimum quantity is also 6 dozen. The prices quoted do not include air freight and insurance.

Full details of various other items and terms can be found in our catalogue and price-list, which we are sending under separate cover.

We hope that you will entrust us with a trial order and look forward to your reply with interest.

                                        Yours truly

                                        P Schmidt
                                        Sales Manager

THE UNDERSMITH CO (EUROPE) AG
12 Gotthardstrasse
6300 Zug, Switzerland

Messrs Woodman & Co
17 Strand
London WIV 7HA   20 June 19..

Dear Sirs,

Electronic Office Systems

Thank you for your inquiry of 14 June. In order to advise you well on the type of equipment that would bring you advantages, we should know more about your type of business, your organization and the paperwork or records it needs, and what contracts, correspondence and reports are generally written. Meanwhile we can explain two systems:

Electronic GK-211   £910 complete

Any business document can be beautifully typed by means of its daisy wheel. Its 'whispering' sound makes it suitable for small and large offices. A memory for about 8000 characters enables corrections or additions to be made easily, and up to 8 pages of text can be stored.

U 2005 Flexible disk word processor   from £7,352

This universal system can be used for all types of text, statistics, communications and their convenient storage. It consists of a keyboard and video display unit, a high speed electronic printer and disk storage cabinet. Typing is simple and speedy - with a wide choice of typestyles - paragraphs, lists, tabulations and word divisions can be automated, and numerous changes, additions and improvements can be made without retyping the whole document.

Would you like our specialist to advise you on the most suitable equipment for your needs? By copy of this quotation we are asking our London representatives, The Undersmith Co (UK) Ltd, 33 Watling Street, London ECI 2MK, to get in touch with you.

                              Yours faithfully

                              Sidney Stevens
                              Manager, Word Processing

cc: London office

artifical silk	*Kunstseide*
parcel	*Paket*
beforehand	*vorgängig, zuvor*
in due course	*zur gegebenen Zeit*
refer to, to	*sich beziehen auf*
fob/free on board	*franko Schiff*
item	*Artikel*
regret, to	*bedauern*
cif/cost, insurance, freight	*Kosten, Versicherung und Fracht inbegriffen*
effect, to	*ausführen*
forwarding agent	*Spediteur*
charges	*(Un)Kosten*
cash with order (CWO)	*Vorausbezahlung, bar bei Bestellung*
cash on delivery (COD)	*bar bei Lieferung, gegen Nachnahme*
rise, to	*steigen*
entrust with, to	*betrauen mit*
trial order	*Probeauftrag*
firm offer	*verbindliches Angebot*
word processor	*Schreibautomat*
daisy wheel	*Druckrad*
whispering	*flüsternd*
character	*Zeichen*
flexible	*flexibel, beweglich*
disk	*Scheibe (hier: Plattenspeicher)*
storage	*Lagerung*
keyboard	*Tastatur*
video display unit	*Bildschirm*
tabulate, to	*tabellarisch (an)ordnen*
automate, to	*automatisieren*
addition	*Zusatz*

Model sentences (quotations)

1 In reply to your enquiry of 8 May, we enclose our detailed quotation and some samples.
2 We were very pleased to receive your einquiry of 21 January and thank you for your interest in our products.
3 We are sure that a trial order will give you full satisfaction and we look forward to hearing from you.
4 You may rely on us to give your order immediate attention.
5 We are certain that our products will meet your requirements.
6 An early reply would help us to despatch your order with the minimum delay.
7 If we have not covered all the points in your inquiry, please do not hesitate to write to us again.
8 The after-sales service we offer is well-known to our customers. You will not be disappointed either.
9 As you see, our prices are very competitive. They are, however, likely to rise, and it is in your interests to place your order as soon as possible.
10 Please let us have your order without delay, since supplies are limited.
11 Our prices are cif Birmingham, covering sea and land transport.
12 If you would prefer to have the goods sent by air freight, this will be charged extra at cost.

	to state	berichten
angeben	to quote	offerieren, zitieren
	to give	geben
	to indicate	anzeigen

Sentences for tranlation

1. Es freut uns, Ihnen unsere günstigsten [= besten] Preise und Zahlungsbedingungen anzugeben.
2. Wir vertrauen darauf, dass wir zu gegebener Zeit eine Bestellung von Ihnen erwarten dürfen.
3. Für grosse Mengen könnten wir Ihnen einen Sonderrabatt von 10% einräumen [= erlauben].
4. Die Sendung, die wir gestern erhalten haben, entspricht nicht den Anforderungen.
5. Der billigste Weg, diesen Probeauftrag zu versenden, ist per Paketpost.
6. Wir können diesen Artikel zu konkurrenzfähigen Preisen bereitstellen und ohne Verzögerung verschicken.
7. Da dies Ihre erste Bestellung ist, sind unsere Bedingungen entweder Vorauszahlung [= «bar bei [with] Bestellung»] oder Nachnahme [= «bar bei [on] Lieferung»].
8. Falls wir Ihre Anfrage nicht zu Ihrer Befriedigung beantwortet haben, zögern Sie bitte nicht, uns erneut zu schreiben.
9. Wir stellen Ihnen einige Muster unseres besten Qualitätsplastiks gesondert zu.
10. Unser Spediteur wird die Kosten für Fracht und Versicherung von Birmingham nach Tel Aviv berechnen.
11. Weitere Einzelheiten über Versand- und Lieferfristen können Sie auf der beigelegten Liste finden.
12. Die Spectraplastics sind leider nicht mehr vorrätig.

Letters for translation

1. Von: Morris Motors Ltd, 66 Prior Street, Oxford OX6 7BR
   An: Herrn Victor S. Sims, Import Agent, Nicosia, Cyprus
   27. März 19..

   Sehr geehrter Herr Sims

   Wir freuen uns (zu erfahren), dass Sie an unseren Morris-Modellen interessiert sind. Wir danken Ihnen für Ihre Anfrage und stellen Ihnen unseren neuesten Katalog sowie einige Faltprospekte gesondert zu.

Der Morris Fortuna ist hier sehr erfolgreich, und auch die grösseren Modelle ziehen in allen Teilen Europas mehr und mehr Kunden an. Unsere Exportpreise sind immer noch vorteilhaft und die Lieferfristen nicht allzu lang. Gerne erwarten wir Ihre Antwort.

Mit freundlichen Grüssen

2. Von: The Undersmith Co (Europe) AG, 12 Gotthardstrasse, 6300 Zug
   An: Electra (European) Holding Corp, 27 rue de Glaciers, 1004 Lausanne

   8. Februar 19..

   Sehr geehrte Herren

   Wir freuen uns, diesem Brief ein Angebot über die Lieferung von 40 Schreibmaschinen beizulegen.
   Da diese Maschinen an Lager sind, können wir sie nach Erhalt Ihrer Bestellung ohne Verzögerung liefern.
   Unsere Maschinen sind aus bestem Qualitätsmaterial hergestellt, so dass sie Ihnen sicher viele Jahre gute Dienste leisten [= geben] werden.
   Wir haben Ihnen unsere besten Bedingungen für diese Menge angegeben.
   Da die Preise unserer Produkte steigen, empfehlen wir Ihnen dringend, Ihre Bestellung noch diesen Monat zu tätigen.

   Mit freundlichen Grüssen

Letter writing assignments

1. Ihre Firma, die Fahrräder produziert, hat eine Anfrage von Mundani & Son aus Karachi, Pakistan, erhalten, die gerne Velos importieren möchte.
   Verfassen Sie eine Antwort, der ein Katalog sowie eine Preisliste mit Geschäftsbedingungen beigelegt ist. Sie hoffen auf einen vielversprechenden Fahrradmarkt in Pakistan und erwarten mit Interesse eine Antwort.

2. Write a quotation for sports shoes from Walkwell Footwear Co of Northampton, England to Showsport Shoe Company, acknowledging their inquiry of the 13th, and enclosing an illustrated catalogue with price-list. Draw the prospective customers' attention to the quality of their walking shoes, which Walkwell have manufactured for forty years. Another line, the Wanderer shoes and boots, are also very popular in England and well-known for their durability. Walkwell have agents in Germany (name and address) in case further information is required. A trial order will have full attention.

6 Offers and firm offers

In many cases a seller will offer goods to regular customers or to new customers, without having received an inquiry, especially when he wants to draw attention to a range of goods, a certain product, or to services and benefits he can give – almost like a sales letter. This is called a voluntary offer. In other cases there may be a special offer of merchandise at a very reasonable price, particularly if the buyer places his order at once.

In general practice offers can be made in these ways

1 a firm offer: the price is valid for a limited period,
2 an offer subject to goods being unsold:
   there is no obligation to supply the goods if they have already been sold elsewhere,
3 an offer subject to confirmation:
   price and delivery time may be changed if necessary.

firm offer	*verbindliches Angebot*
regular customer	*Stammkunde, regelmässiger Kunde*
merchandise	*Ware*
valid	*gültig*
limited	*beschränkt, begrenzt*
subject to	*abhängig von, vorbehältlich*
subj. to goods being unsold	*Zwischenverkauf vorbehalten*
obligation	*Verpflichtung*
subj. to confirmation	*Bestätigung vorbehalten*

Vocabulary exercise

Choose the correct words from the list.

1 Goods are often ____ without a customer having made an ____.
2 Sometimes the seller has a ____ of goods, or he wants to ____ to a new product.
3 An offer may be made to new or ____ customers and is in many ways like a ____ letter.
4 The seller lets a ____ buyer know if he can sell ____ at a ____ price.
5 In such cases the buyer should ____ his order soon, especially if the offer is ____ to goods being ____.
6 A ____ offer is one quoting prices that are ____ for a certain time only.
7 When price and ____ time may be changed, the offer is made subject to ____.

confirmation
delivery
draw attention
firm
inquiry
merchandise
offered
place
prospective
range
reasonable
regular
sales
subject
unsold
valid

Note: Various forms of layout are shown in the following letters.

THE STATE SUPPLIERS INC.
419 West Street   Houston, Texas 83192

International Traders Inc.
56 Central Street
Seattle, Washington 98122   November 15, 19..

Subject: 'SIESTA' deck chairs

Gentlemen:

We welcome your inquiry about deck chairs and are pleased to submit our lowest prices in the enclosed quotation.

The chairs asked for are in heavy demand at present. Because we are booking a great many orders, we would point out that this quotation is subject to the goods being unsold.

We are confident that both the quality of our chairs, which can be supplied from stock, and our terms, as shown on the enclosed quotation, will give you complete satisfaction.

                                           Very truly yours
                                           STATE SUPPLIERS INC.

                                           Charles S. Gibson
                                           Marketing Manager

Enc: Quotation No 321/s
       Leaflet G
CSG: jn

THE STATE SUPPLIERS INC.
419 West Street   Houston, Texas 83192

QUOTATION

The International Traders Inc.
56 Central Street
Seattle, Washington 98122   November 15, 19..

	Quantity	Price
'SIESTA' deck chairs	up to 100	$8.00 each
illustrated in leaflet G	101 - 250	$7.25 each
enclosed	251 - 500	$6.75 each

CONDITIONS OF SALE

General	All sales are subject to acceptance of following conditions and terms.
Prices	All quotations for orders are subject to prices valid at date of dispatch.
Delivery time	Immediately from stock, subject to goods being unsold.
Delivery charges	We pay freight inside US on all orders to the amount of one hundred dollars and over. For orders under one hundred dollars in value we charge for freight at cost.
Terms of payment	Inside US: Payment should be made within 30 days from date of invoice. Abroad: Payment through a New York bank on receipt of shipping documents.

State Suppliers Inc.

PEDRO ESCUDERA & CO

P.O. Box 4, Valencia, Espana

Fresh Fruit Wholesalers, Ltd.,
14 King Street,
Covent Garden,
London WC1 Y06   4th December 19..

Dear Sirs,

'Goldglow' Oranges

 We appreciate your interest in our 'Goldglow' oranges, about which you inquired on 27th November. You will find that our prices compare favourably with those of our competitors. We quote as follows:

 'Goldglow' Medium £3.12 per cwt. (50kg)
 'Goldglow' Large £4.10 per cwt. (50kg)

 These prices are firm, subject to our receiving your order not later than December 31, 19... They include delivery fob Valencia and are valid for a minimum of 3 tons. If your order should exceed 10 tons we can grant you 5% discount. Packing free.

 Terms of payment: 90 days' sight draft.
 Time of delivery: First half of January next.

 You will be receiving a small sample case of 'Goldglow' oranges by air mail next week. If you entrust us with an initial order, as we hope you will, you may rely on our following your shipping instructions carefully.

              Yours faithfully

LIGHTSON LIGHTERS PTY
6th Floor, Saint Martin's Tower
31 Market Street
Sydney NSW 2000
Australia

The Madison Stores
319 Fifth Avenue
New York, NY 10010
USA

August 21, 19..

Gentlemen:

Two years ago we had the pleasure of supplying you with our Lightson lighters. We trust that your customers were satisfied with the styles and our guaranteed quality.

On this occasion we would draw your attention to our greatly reduced prices. We have brought out our stainless steel lighter in four new styles, and are able to make you a special offer, which is valid up to the end of September of this year. The retailers' prices listed are subject to a trade discount of 4% on all orders received during this period. We are confident that you will take advantage of these terms to replenish your stocks in time for the Christmas trade. The enclosed photographs show how attractive our new styles are - two new ladies' lighters and two new gentlemen's lighters.

Of course, the models you purchased previously are still available, as you will see from the latest price-list enclosed. As you may remember, all our lighters are shipped after receipt of confirmation that a Letter of Credit has been opened with the ABC Bank of Australia.

Kindly remember: our offer expires on September 30, so why not order now?

Sincerely yours

LIGHTSON LIGHTERS PTY

Enc

submit, to	vorlegen, unterbreiten
in heavy demand	stark gefragt
confident	zuversichtlich
compare favourably with	günstig abschneiden im Vergleich mit
competitor	Konkurrent
exceed, to	übersteigen, übertreffen
sight draft	Sichtwechsel
case	Kiste
initial	erste
lighter	Feuerzeug
reduce, to	vermindern, reduzieren
stainless	rostfrei
retailer	Detaillist, Einzelhändler
take advantage of, to	Gebrauch machen von
replenish, to	ergänzen, (wieder) auffüllen
purchase, to	kaufen
previously	früher, vorher
expire, to	verfallen, ablaufen

Model sentences (offers)

1. The demand for our sports shoes has been increasing rapidly in your country.
2. These shoes can be supplied in three qualities and in five colours.
3. You will be interested to know that we have just introduced our new range of wallpapers in the latest designs.
4. We have pleasure in offering you the following goods for immediate delivery.
5. This offer is subject to goods being unsold on receipt of your order.
6. We can supply the jackets on very favourable terms.
7. As we are quoting a special price on this occasion, the offer is not subject to the usual discounts.
8. As prices are likely to rise, it is in your own interest to place your order as soon as possible.
9. For orders of 100 or more we can allow a special discount of 4%.
10. All prices are reduced by 10 per cent during the month of January.
11. Please let us have your order by the end of next week, since supplies are limited.
12. The prices are firm until the end of this year, but delivery is subject to the availability of raw materials.
13. Please let us know your requirements by completing the order form.

Sentences for translation

1. Beiliegend finden Sie unseren Prospekt samt Preisliste.
2. Falls uns Ihre Muster gefallen, werden wir ansehnliche Bestellungen vornehmen können.
3. Unser Angebot gilt, (zwischenzeitlicher) Verkauf der Ware vorbehalten, sobald wir Ihre Bestellung erhalten.

4. Wir sind zuversichtlich, dass unsere Artikel im Vergleich mit denen unserer Konkurrenz günstig abschneiden.
5. Dieses Angebot ist bis zum Monatsende verbindlich.
6. Ihre Artikel erfüllen unsere Anforderungen.
7. Unsere Preise könnten steigen; deshalb raten wir Ihnen, eine Bestellung bald vorzunehmen.
8. Wir können diese Lampen ab Lager innert einer Woche liefern.
9. Schon seit dem 1. Juli haben wir einen Rabatt von 5% gewährt.
10. In unserem Brief vom 10. dieses Monats betonten wir, dass das Angebot unter Vorbehalt einer Bestätigung gilt und dass wir eine frühzeitige Antwort erwarten.
11. Da unsere Vorräte beschränkt sind, werden Preisänderungen möglich sein.
12. Unser Vertreter wird in Kürze die englischen Grossisten besuchen, um ihnen unsere Produkte zu zeigen.

Letters for translation

1. An: Hooper & Adams, 39 Commissioner Street, Johannesburg, South Africa

    11. November 19..

    Danke für Ihre Anfrage vom 2. November; beiliegend senden wir Ihnen unseren neuesten illustrierten Katalog. Artikel 1–14 können sofort geliefert werden, die andern innert 4 Wochen nach Erhalt Ihrer Bestellung.
    Unsere Zahlungsbedingungen finden Sie auf der gelben Liste.
    Wir sind zuversichtlich, dass Sie die angebotenen Artikel voll befriedigen werden. Wir möchten ganz speziell Ihre Aufmerksamkeit auf Nr. 13, 15 und 16 lenken, und wir erwarten gerne Ihre erste Bestellung, die wir mit grosser Sorgfalt ausführen werden.

2. An: George Thompson & Cie, zHv. Frau Alice Bugnon, 26 route Riaz, 1630 Bulle

    23. Januar 19..

    Sehr geehrte Frau Bugnon

    In Beantwortung Ihrer Anfrage vom 20. Januar senden wir Ihnen mit separater Post unseren Katalog mit Detailhandelspreisen für Schreibmaschinen. Diese Preise sind zwei Monate gültig.
    Unsere Werbung hat Ihnen bereits eine Vorstellung [= Idee] von der ausgezeichneten Qualität unserer Schreibmaschinen vermittelt. Wir können Ihnen mehrere Modelle anbieten: portable, mechanische, elektrische und elektronische Schreibmaschinen. Sie werden sicher ein Modell finden, das Ihren Erfordernissen entspricht.
    Sie werden zugeben müssen, dass unsere Preise konkurrenzfähig sind, und so hoffen wir, von Ihnen bald eine Bestellung zu erhalten.

Letter writing assignments

1. The motor vehicle factory, British Leyland Ltd of Coventry, England, writes a circular to all existing customers in Middlesex, England, announcing that an agent has been appointed there for Morris and BMC cars. This is: Carters Car Centre, 1 Hill Road, Harrow, Middx., Tel: 01 7358964.
They can supply most new models from stock, trade in secondhand cars, and are well-equipped to give good service. Invite customers to go and see the latest models in the Carters showrooms. They are sure to find a good car there which will give them trouble-free use and great satisfaction.

2. Ihr Unternehmen stellt Fahrräder her. Verfassen Sie ein Rundschreiben an amerikanische Händler, in dem Sie Ihr Standardmodell zu einem – auf einen Monat befristeten – Einführungspreis anbieten. Beginnen Sie Ihren Brief mit einem zugkräftigen Absatz, der auf die grosse Beliebtheit des Velofahrens in der heutigen Zeit verweist.

7 Orders

When a prospective buyer has received and compared the quotations and offers he has received, he will be ready to place an order. This is quite a straightforward matter. He usually uses his own order form, or one sent him by the supplier. Very often too, a salesman or representative calling on the customer will complete the order form for him to sign.

A private person who places orders infrequently, or a small company, may place the order in the form of a letter. Letters also have to be written to give special instructions, to express certain conditions and to ask questions. And an order may be combined with a counter-offer too.

straightforward	einfach
order form	Bestellformular
in the form of	in Form von
infrequently	unregelmässig, hie und da
express, to	ausdrücken
counter-offer	Gegenofferte

Vocabulary exercise

Choose the correct words from the list.
1. The goods will be dispatched after ____ of confirmation that a letter of ____ has been opened at a bank.
2. Our offer is ____ till 31 March.
3. All sales are subject to ____ of the following ____.
4. We are confident that you will take ____ of these conditions to replenish your ____.
5. A buyer usually receives several ____ which he should ____.
6. It is a ____ procedure to ____ an order form.
7. Often the customer just ____ the order presented by the ____.
8. Small ____ may place their order by letter and combine it with a ____-offer.

acceptance
advantage
companies
compare
complete
counter
credit
quotations
receipt
salesman
signs
stocks
straightforward
terms
valid

55

SEARS, THORNTON & CO

Rhodes Square
Marare Zimbabwe

Caran d'Ache
1200 Geneva
Switzerland

22 February 19..

Export Order for Pencils

Dear Sirs

We have received your catalogue and samples, which you sent under cover of your letter of 14th of this month. After testing the pencils we are pleased to state that they give full satisfaction and we therefore request you to supply:

5000 gross Pencils HB at Sfr 9.90 per dozen fob Genoa on the terms quoted in your letter mentioned above.

Shipping instructions will be sent you by our forwarding agents, Messrs Guardi & Co of Genoa, Italy. Please let us have your invoice in duplicate.

If this first order is carried out satisfactorily, it will almost certainly lead to repeat orders.

Yours faithfully

LONDON SCHOOL OF BUSINESS STUDIES

14 Russell Square
London WC1 ZX3

The Undersmith Co (Europe) AG
12 Gotthardstrasse
6300 Zug
Switzerland   2 July 19..

Dear Sirs

Thank you for your quotation of 17 June and for placing your word processor U 2005 at our disposal. Several members of our staff attended your demonstration and have since tested the equipment. We have found that it is versatile and simple to operate, and so it is suitable for our needs at school and for instruction purposes.

Therefore we wish to order:
One U 2005 Flexible disk word processor comprising the following units
- Screen for sharp and clear characters dispayed in green on a dark background large enough for 28 lines of 80 characters each, plus 3 control lines
- Keyboard with 96 keys, repeat automat for all keys and storage unit
- Printer for programmed line spacing and a typing speed of 2,700 characters per minute
- Disks with a capacity of 127 pages (300,000 characters) each
- Software according to your specification.

Price complete Sfr 24,000, CIF London, including installation.
Delivery within 6 weeks.
Guarantee: 6 months, after which we shall sign a service contract at Sfr 2,100 per annum.

Yours faithfully

Keith Henderson BA
Director

               The Hutton Wholesalers Ltd
               125 King William Sreet
                  London EC4 3PJ

Master Watches S.A.
2400 Le Locle
Suisse
                                        28 March 19..

att: Mr P Schmidt

Dear Sirs

We acknowledge receipt fo your letter of 14 March and have
pleasure in enclosing our Order No PMB-581 for Mod. 05 for
your prompt and careful execution.

To our regret we cannot yet place an order for Mod. 07, because we think the price quoted rather high. We would ask
you to reduce this price of Sfr 420 to Sfr 380 a dozen, as
there is quite some competition on the market.

Please let us know when the goods are ready for shipment.
We shall then let you have our final shipping instructions.

                              Yours faithfully

                              THE HUTTON WHOLESALERS LTD

                              F Winston
                              Chief Buyer

Your ref: PS:lt
Our ref: FW:JD

Enc: Order

suit, to	entsprechen, sich eignen zu/für
need	Bedürfnis
carriage paid	franco
note, to	Kenntnis nehmen von
state, to	feststellen
invoice	Rechnung
in duplicate	im Doppel
execute an order, to	eine Bestellung ausführen
repeat order	Nachbestellung, neuerliche Bestellung
acknowledge, to	bestätigen, zugeben
execution (of an order)	Ausführung
quite some	ziemlich viel
shipment	Lieferung
final	definitiv

Model sentences (orders)

1. Please supply the undermentioned goods for immediate delivery.
2. We would like to know if air freight and insurance are included in the price quoted.
3. We have pleasure in placing an order with you for the articles specified below.
4. Kindly arrange for the supply of the following articles.
5. Please confirm that you can supply this quantity by 24 April.
6. Following our telephone conversation this morning, please despatch the following records to us by rail.
7. Would you kindly send me the free reprint 'New Dimensions in Sound Recording', which you offered on last night's radio broadcast.
8. As we are nearly out of stock of these articles, we urge you to deliver them on time.
9. If you cannot send us the articles ordered on the dates mentioned, please supply a suitable substitute.
10. We have pleasure in enclosing our Order No 225/WG, and would ask you to return the duplicate to us, duly signed, as an acknowledgement.

Sentences for translation

1. Wir bestätigen den Empfang Ihrer Offerte vom 15. März.
2. Wir freuen uns, Ihnen eine Probebestellung zu den in Ihrem Schreiben erwähnten Bedingungen aufzugeben.
3. Wir bitten Sie, uns einen bebilderten Prospekt jener Stühle zuzustellen, welche Sie innert drei Wochen beschaffen können.
4. Unsere Bestellung Nr.... für ... liegt bei.
5. Danke für Ihre Muster. Wir würden jetzt gerne bestellen ...
6. Bitte fertigen Sie folgendes per Zug ab ...
7. Im Anschluss an unser Telefongespräch vom ... liefern Sie bitte ...
8. Wollen Sie (uns) bitte die unten erwähnten Waren umgehend [= mit minimaler Verzögerung] zuschicken.

9. Bitte benachrichtigen Sie uns, sobald die Güter versandt worden sind.
10. Schnelle Erledigung dieser Bestellung wird sehr geschätzt.
11. Wir wären dankbar, wenn wir die Waren früher erhalten könnten.
12. Wir rechnen damit [= vertrauen darauf], dass Sie dieser Bestellung Ihre unmittelbare Aufmerksamkeit widmen [= geben] werden.

Letters for translation

An: Pedro Escudera & Co., Postbus 41, Valencia, Spanien

19. Dezember 19..

Wir haben Ihre Mustersendung erhalten, die Sie uns zu Beginn des Monats gesandt haben, und möchten nun gerne einen Probeauftrag erteilen:

10 Tonnen «Goldglow» grosse Orangen zu £ 4.50 je Zentner, franko Schiff Valencia

Rabatt:	5%
Verpackung:	kostenlos
Zahlungsbedingungen:	90 Tage nach Sicht
Versand:	bis spätestens 10. Januar 19..

Wir erteilen Ihnen diesen Auftrag nur unter der Bedingung, dass die Ware bis allerspätestens am 10. Januar versandt wird. Unsere Verschiffungsanweisungen werden Ihnen demnächst durch unsere Spediteure Stewart & Kerns, 22 Upper Thames Street, London EC1B 3DQ zugestellt. Bitte bestätigen Sie (uns) das genaue Lieferdatum.
The Holborn Bank wird Ihnen gerne jede gewünschte Auskunft über unsere Firma geben.
Wir hoffen, dass eine sorgfältige Ausführung dieses Auftrages zu regelmässigen Geschäftsbeziehungen führen wird.

                                                Fresh Fruit Wholesalers

Letter writing assignments

1. Sie arbeiten in einer Buchhandlung, die nun dringend 400 Englisch-Sprachbücher «Let's go» benötigt.
   Bestellen Sie den Titel beim Verlag Longman in Harlow, England.
   Die Bücher müssen am 20. August in Ihrem Besitz sein, da eine Woche später das neue Schuljahr beginnt.
2. Write a letter to D'Arcy Fashions, 13 Mortimer Street, London WL8 34C, referring to their representative's visit last week. Order certain ladies' or gentlemen's clothes (giving quantity, catalogue number and price), stating which alternatives would be accepted if any are not in stock, and asking for prompt delivery.

8 Status inquiries and references

Supplying a quantity of goods to a customer on credit is a matter of trust. Business and trade would be unthinkable nowadays without the facilities of credit allowed for a certain period (generally 10–30 days for inland trade, 60–90 days for export and import). In the case of a new customer, a supplier's credit manager usually tries to find out whether he is trustworthy by making inquiries about his financial standing. This can be done in three ways:

1 Taking up trade references by writing to other suppliers.
2 Asking the bank to make status inquiries or to obtain financial information.
3 Using the services of an inquiry agency.

Until the information has been obtained, goods may be supplied to a new customer on a cash with order basis, or by requesting cash on delivery. This procedure is, however, more complicated.

1 Trade references are usually given by another supplier of the new customer. If the payments have been made promptly, this supplier will certainly give a good reference. But if bills are paid slowly, or only after the supplier sends several reminders, then the information will be unfavourable.
However, a company providing an unsatisfactory reference has to be very careful. If such a letter falls into wrong hands, or the information is proved to be false, a costly lawsuit for libel may be the result. Look at letter p. 66 and see how cautious the writer has been in giving an adverse report on his customer. He has not even mentioned the customer's name in his letter.

2 Bank references are also couched in rather cautious terms. A credit manager is, however, used to receiving such correspondence, and can read between the lines and interpret the message.

3 An inquiry agency charges fees for its services. As forms are used for such inquiries and replies, they have not been included in this book.

Note: Businessmen also make inquiries of a more personal nature concerning a new business relationship.

status inquiry	*Bonitätsauskunft, Erkundigung*
trust	*Vertrauen*
facility	*Möglichkeit*
trustworthy	*vertrauenswürdig*
standing	*Ruf, Ansehen*
financial standing	*Vermögenslage*
take up references, to	*Referenzen ermitteln*
obtain, to	*erlangen*
inquiry agency	*Auskunftei*

complicated	*kompliziert*
reminder	*Mahnung*
prompt	*umgehend*
unfavourable	*ungünstig*
provide, to	*beliefern*
unsatisfactory	*unbefriedigend*
lawsuit	*Prozess*
libel	*Verleumdung*
cautious	*vorsichtig*
adverse	*ungünstig*
couch, to	*in Worte fassen*
interpret, to	*auslegen*
fee	*Honorar*
concerning	*betreffend*
business relationship	*Geschäftsbeziehung*

Vocabulary exercise

Choose the correct words from the list.
1 A supplier has to ____ customers when he sends goods on ____.
2 To make sure if the new customer is ____ the credit manager must make ____ about his financial ____.
3 Trade references can be given by another ____.
4 A bank can also make ____ inquiries.
5 A third possibility is to apply to an ____ for information.
6 A good ____ can be given by another supplier if ____ are made promptly.
7 However, if he has had to write several ____ his information will be ____.
8 When replying negatively the writer has to be very ____, otherwise he could be taken court for ____.

agency
cautious
credit
inquiries
libel
payments
reference
reminders
standing
status
supplier
trust
trustworthy
unsatisfactory

UNDERSMITH TYPEWRITER CO., INC.
52 THIRD AVENUE, CLEVELAND, OHIO 44133

Messrs. Farmer & Co.
Broad Street
Toronto, Canada

February 17, 19..

Gentlemen:

We were very pleased to receive your order for goods to the value Can $2,000.00

Since we have not done business with you so far, will you kindly furnish us with the names of firms or a bank to whom we can apply for a reference. As soon as these inquiries have been satisfactorily answered we shall be pleased to dispatch the goods and open a credit account for future business.

We trust that this will be the beginning of a pleasant business association.

Very truly yours

UNDERSMITH TYPEWRITER CO. INC.

Enc: Order acknowledgement

UNDERSMITH TYPEWRITER CO., INC.
52 THIRD AVENUE, CLEVELAND, OHIO 44133

CONFIDENTIAL

Messrs. Temperton Bros.
1012 Pacific Avenue
Toronto, Ontario
Canada

February 21, 19..

Gentlemen:

Your name has been given to us by Messrs. Farmer & Co of Toronto, who have placed an order with us for goods to the value of Can $2,000.00

Would you kindly give us your opinion regarding their reputation and financial standing. We shall, of course, treat your advice in strict confidence.

With many thanks in advance for your assistance.

Very truly yours

UNDERSMITH TYPEWRITER CO. INC.

Temperton Bros, 17 Parliament Avenue, Toronto, Ontario

CONFIDENTIAL

The Undersmith Typewriter Co Inc
Accounts Department
52 Third Avenue
Cleveland, Ohio 44133

February 26, 19..

Gentlemen:

We are pleased to answer your inquiry of February 21 concerning

Messrs Farmer & Co, Broad Street, Toronto.

They have been regular customers of ours for the last ten years, and we regard them as being most reliable and trustworthy. Our opinion is that you can allow a credit of $2,000 without any risk, as the turnover we have with them is in excess of this amount and they have always met their liabilities promptly.

This information is, of course, given without responsibility on our part.

Sincerely yours

Burroughs Business Machines Inc., Chicago, Illinois 60615
110 Grand Avenue

STRICTLY CONFIDENTIAL

The Undersmith Typewriter Co.Inc.
Accounts Department
52 Third Avenue
Cleveland, Ohio 44133

February 26, 19..

Subject: Your inquiry of Feb. 21, 19..

Gentlemen:

The firm whose name is shown on the enclosed slip has been a customer of ours for two years. The orders placed with us have been less in value than the amount you mention, and accounts were usually settled slowly, some only after we had made several requests for payment.

Although the reputation of these customers is generally considered to be good, we should hesitate to supply goods for this amount other than on a cash basis.

This information is for your own use only and is given without responsibility.

Yours truly

Enc

UNDERSMITH TYPEWRITER CO., INC.
52 THIRD AVENUE, CLEVELAND, OHIO 44133

CONFIDENTIAL

The Manager
First National Bank Inc.
Albington, Ohio 51032

February 21, 19..

Dear Sir:

Messrs. Farmer & Co. of Toronto, Canada, have given us the name of their bank:

Commonwealth Bank of Canada, West Park, Toronto as a reference.

This company has placed a trial order to the value of $2,000.00. Would you kindly advise us whether this credit can safely be granted.

We should be grateful fo any additional information you could give us about their business methods and reputation.

Very truly yours

UNDERSMITH TYPEWRITER CO. INC.

First National Bank Inc.
43 Commercial Road
Albington, Illinois 51032

PRIVATE AND CONFIDENTIAL

Mr. Harold P. Mason
Accounts Department
The Undersmith Typewriter Co.Inc.
Cleveland, Ohio 44133

                                        February 28, 19..

Dear Mr. Mason:

We have now received information from the bank in Toronto, for which you asked us in your letter of February 21.

The firm you inquired about was established in 1950. During the first years of trading profits were satisfactory, but these have decreased lately.

Caution is recommended in allowing a credit of $2,000.

Please regard this information as strictly private and without responsibility.

                                        Sincerely yours

Walkwell Footwear plc Northampton N19 3AF
35 Wellington Square   England

Hans Johanssen Esq
10 Fredensgade
Copenhagen, Denmark   1 April 19..

Dear Sir

We wish to appoint an agent for the sale of our shoes in Denmark. A business acquaintance of yours, Mr Nils Andersen of Copenhagen, has offered us his services, giving your name as a referee.

Would you be so kind as to give us some information regarding his suitability as an agent, his business reputation and financial standing.

We assure you that we shall treat your information in strict confidence, and thank you sincerely in advance.

                                Yours faithfully

                                WALKWELL FOOTWEAR

Enc: International
     Reply Paid Coupon

acknowledgement	Bestätigung
furnish with, to	ausstatten mit
apply to, to	ersuchen, beantragen
association	Verbindung
confidential	vertraulich
regarding	betreffend
treat, to	behandeln
in confidence	vertraulich
assistance	Hilfe, Beistand
regard, to	betrachten
reliable	zuverlässig
turnover	Umsatz
be in excess of, to	überschreiten
meet one's liabilities	seinen Verpflichtungen/Schulden nachkommen
responsibility	Verantwortung
on our part	unsererseits
on a cash basis	gegen bar
grant, to	gewähren
grateful	dankbar
additional	zusätzlich
establish, to	gründen
profit	Gewinn
decrease, to	abnehmen, sinken
lately	neuerdings
caution	Vorsicht
recommend, to	empfehlen
acquaintance	Bekanntschaft, Bekannte(r)
referee	Referent, Schiedsrichter
suitability	Eignung

Model sentences (status inquiries and references)

1. The BPD Company has given us your name as a reference.
2. We have not yet had any business dealings with this company, and would be very grateful if you could give us some information on their financial standing.
3. Would you let us know if you consider that a credit of ... can be allowed without risk?
4. Can you inform us about their reputation in your area?
5. Thank you in advance for any information that you may be able to give us.
6. Your reply will, of course, be treated strictly confidentially.
7. The company about whom you inquire is well-known in our branch.
8. Messrs B&D have been regular customers of ours for three years.
9. We are pleased to inform you that the firm referred to in your inquiry of ... has always met its commitments promptly.
10. In our opinion you would run no risk granting credit in the amount you mention.
11. As we have not done a great deal of business with them, we cannot give you very reliable information.

12 We regret that we are unable to give you the information you require.
13 In reply to your status inquiry of ..., we would recommend dealing with the customer in question on a cash basis only.
14 We would advise caution in your dealings with this company.
15 This information is given in strict confidence and without responsibility on our part.

Sentences for translation

1. Wollen Sie uns bitte die Namen zweier Firmen (an)geben, die wir um Referenzen ersuchen können?
2. Wenn unsere Erkundigungen zur Zufriedenheit beantwortet sind, werden wir gerne ein Kreditkonto für zukünftige Geschäfte eröffnen.
3. Könnten Sie uns mitteilen, ob diese Firma ihre Zahlungen pünktlich erledigt [= macht]?
4. In Beantwortung Ihrer Anfrage vom 17. Januar verweisen wir Sie an unsere Bank und an zwei Unternehmen, mit denen wir regelmässig Geschäfte tätigen.
5. Besteht ein Risiko beim Einräumen eines Kredites über diesen Betrag?
6. Wir sehen Ihrer Antwort entgegen.
7. Die XYZ Unternehmung ist seit zehn Jahren unser Kunde.
8. Soweit wir wissen, ist ihr finanzieller Ruf gut.
9. Wir denken, dass Sie den verlangten Kredit gefahrlos einräumen [= erlauben] können.
10. Sie sind langsam im Begleichen ihrer Verpflichtungen.
11. Wir haben kürzlich gehört, dass sie finanzielle Schwierigkeiten haben.
12. Unter diesen Umständen würden wir zögern, ihnen Kredit im erwähnten Betrag einzuräumen [= erlauben].
13. Ihre Gewinne sind neuerdings zurückgegangen.
14. Bitte betrachten Sie diese Auskunft als streng vertraulich und unverbindlich [= ohne Verantwortung unsererseits] gegeben.

Letters for translation

Von: The BPD Company, 20 Camden Road, Brighton BR7 2AA
An: Undersmith Co (UK) plc, 33 Watling Street, London EC1 2MK   VERTRAULICH
20. September 19..

In Ihrem Schreiben vom 18. September baten Sie uns um Auskunft über das St. Andrew's College.
Die Vermögenslage der Schule kennen wir nicht; das College besitzt jedoch in Brighton einen sehr guten Ruf. Es wurde 1945 gegründet und hat über 1000 Schüler.

Wir haben für diese Schule verschiedene grössere Bestellungen ausgeführt, und sie ist ihren Verpflichtungen immer pünktlich nachgekommen. Wir glauben daher, dass ein Kredit von £ 1,800 gefahrlos gewährt werden kann.
Wir erteilen [= geben] Ihnen die Auskunft ohne Verbindlichkeit unsererseits.

Letter writing assignments

1   You are the English correspondent of the Fantastic Furniture Factory, 41–45 Industriestrasse, 5001 Aarau.
    You have received an order for furniture in the value of nearly £ 12,000 from the Harris Import Company of Hull HU2 3CG England. They have given the name of the Erisexport Ltd Nordgade, Bergen, Sweden as a reference.
    Write the status inquiry.

2   Write a reply from Erisexport Ltd advising against allowing such a large credit, giving reasons.

9 Office automation (I): the word processor

The typewriter as we know it has been in existence for more than a hundred years. Its extensive use in offices at the beginning of this century made it possible for women to enter the field of business – formerly men's domain. Although it brought many advantages, as most automation did, typewriting also led to dull work with little variety.
To do something about that and to save work and expense in producing standard letters, many such letters and forms too were printed and duplicated. However, as the quantity of printed material increased, people in offices began to sort their mail. They put aside printed paper, duplicated circulars and so on, giving more interest to 'proper letters'. So ways had to be found to produce individually addressed and typed letters that would receive attention.

The word processor

The answer to the problem was word processing. With the help of a word processor letters, reports and other documents can be typed as a draft or in their final form and shown on a screen. When mistakes have to be corrected, when changes have to be made or when things have to be added, this can be done very quickly and easily: you simply type them in on the screen again. When the letters etc. are as you want them, they are reproduced by the printer in high quality typing in a few minutes.
But there is more. What a word processor can also do is:

- control the length of lines and pages
- centre titles
- indicate paragraphs and headings
- divide words at the end of a line
- arrange columns and tables
- fill in forms
- leave out and put in parts.

As said before, there is a great deal of duplication in routine correspondence. Numerous letters of a company contain sentences and paragraphs that are written over and over again and require only a few individual additions, such as the customer's name and address, prices and dates, for example.
In this connection too, the word processor is very useful for it can well be used for programmed correspondence. A member of the staff has to analyse the letters and documents, which are typical for the company or certain departments, for standard paragraphs. These paragraphs are typed into a memory medium – a magnetic tape or a disk – and kept for future use. There are spaces for the individual parts (names, prices etc.) to be typed as required. All paragraphs are numbered, and together they form a paragraph selection catalogue.
The paragraphs can now be retrieved when wanted – for a certain quotation for instance – and the printer will again produce without any mistake, high quality letters at a high speed (550 words a minute). Another memory unit is used for the letter elements that are not always the same, but vary with different letters, so that they can also be retrieved and used when needed.

Using the word processor in this way, some organizations have found that they can do much more in less time, and in that way save a lot of administration costs.

The many model sentences in this book and the sentences you have translated will help you to compose similar paragraphs for programming.

dull	eintönig
variety	Abwechslung
expense	Ausgabe
form	Formular
duplicate, to	vervielfältigen
sort, to	sortieren
proper	schicklich, anständig
word processing	Textverarbeitung
draft	Entwurf
screen	(Bild)Schirm, Leinwand
centre, to	zentrieren
paragraph	Abschnitt, Absatz
heading	Überschrift
divide, to	trennen
arrange, to	(an)ordnen
column	Kolonne
table	Tabelle
memory	Gedächtnis, (Computer)Speicher
selection	Auswahl
retrieve, to	wiedergewinnen, (hier:) abrufen
unit	Einheit
management	Direktion

Vocabulary exercise

Choose the correct words from the list.
1. The ____ has been a most useful machine in ____ for at least a century.
2. Like most forms of ____ it caused people to do ____ work.
3. An economical way of ____ standard letters was to have them ____ .
4. However, customers began to play less attention to ____ letters, and to show more interest in ____ typed correspondence.
5. Using a word ____ , a typist prepares a ____ which is shown on a screen.
6. After ____ have been made, the printer will ____ it in a perfect form.
7. Typing ____ is no problem either and the word processor can also be set to ____ in forms.
8. Some ____ are repeated in several letters, and need only a few ____ .

additions
automation
changes
columns
draft
dull
duplicated
fill
individually
offices
paragraphs
printed
processor
producing
reproduce
typewriter

Inquiry   Disk 4.21   Programme I 2/329

Code	Subject	Text
00	Address	_____
01	Date	_____
02	Salutation	Dear Sirs
03	"	Dear _____
04	"	Gentlemen:
05	"	Dear Sir or Madam
06	Subject	_____
07	Trade journal	We read your address in the _____
08	Trade fair	We saw your products at the _____
09	Business contact	We have received your address from business friends, _____
10	Business activities	For several years we have dealt in _____
11	Sales intention	In the near future we plan to sell _____ in our range.
12	Request quotation	Would you send us a quotation for _____
13	Illustrations etc.	Would you send us an illustrated catalogue or leaflet with prices, terms and times of delivery.
14	Delivery	Are you able to make delivery within ____ weeks?
15	Best prices	When calculating your quotation, will you please remember that we can do business with you only if you quote competitive prices.
16	Discount	Kindly let us know what discounts you can allow for _____
17	Cash discount	Kindly let us know what discounts you would allow.
18	Your reply	We look forward to your early reply with interest.
19	Close	Yours faithfully
20	Close	Yours sincerely

Rejection of Offer   Disk 855

                        Programme RO 1/120

Code	Subject	Text
01	Salutation	Dear Sirs
02	Thanks Rejection	Thank you for your offer _____. We can, unfortunately not take advantage of it as_____
03	No need	we do not need this material at present.
04	Price too high	the prices are considerably higher than those quoted elsewhere.
05	Del.too long	the delivery times you quote are too long.
06	Quality un-satisfactory	the quality does not come up to our standards.
07	Alternative	If you can make us another offer which is more suitable, we would be pleased to hear from you.
08	Close	Yours faithfully

                        Programme D 3/615

Code	Subject	Text
01	Salutation	Dear Sirs
02	"	Dear _____
03	Reference	Our invoice No _____ of _____
04	"	Our Statement of Account dated _____
05	Thanks payment	Thank you for your payment that we received on __
06	Credit terms	You have, however, not paid the full amount outstanding but have deducted ___% cash discount. This must be an error, because the credit terms we quoted were for ___ payment.
07	Discount period expired	If your payment had reached us before _____ we could have allowed you to deduct the discount, but unfortunately the credit period has expired and the net amount is due to us.
08	Remit remainder	Would you please remit the remainder of _____ within the next few days.
09	Prompt payment in future	Prompt payment of our accounts in future will enable us to grant you the maximum discount; this is in the interest of all concerned.
10	Close	Yours faithfully
11	"	Yours sincerely

Letter writing assignments

1   On the basis of letters and model sentences in Chapter 5 and 6, write a programme for quotations.
2   Referring to page 75, Disk 4.21 write a letter dated 2 November 19.. addressed to Torrson & Sons, Surbrunnengaten 81, 13327 Stockholm, Sweden for office furniture, using these paragraph selections.
    02, 06, 07, 11, 13, 17, 18, 19

Office automation (II): the computer

Strange though it may seem, many people feel a sense of fear when the word "computer" is mentioned. Some even become aggressive, especially when it is suggested they should work with one.

How is it that a piece of equipment, now almost a universal tool in every laboratory, warehouse, office, bank – and indeed in numerous homes – should be feared. Perhaps the idea of a machine taking over a person's work, and the thought of unemployment come to mind; but more of this later.

The computer at its simplest, is a very fast calculating machine, capable of storing vast quantities of data in its electronic memory, and doing countless jobs (programs) at electronic speeds. Material is stored on a tape medium or a disk, and information can be recorded and retrieved for example as on any cassette tape recorder. Practically any task connected with calculating can be processed. There is a huge variety of uses of the computer, complete with display screens, printers and connected equipment.

A computer can complete repetitive functions like printing address labels. Inventory in a warehouse is greatly simplified, as the manual listing and cross-checking are done automatically. Stock leaving is noted, remaining items or those in short supply can be shown on screen or print-out within seconds. Optical readers take over boring writing jobs, and warning notes of when to reorder are handled by the computer: even the reordering itself.

However, before any work is done, the computer must receive its orders or programs. Now comes the first shock – the computer does not understand English. Thus, one of a number of special languages must be mastered. These dialogues – Cobol, Fortran, Algol, Basic or PL/1 to name a few – contain hundreds of elements, and the interested user can soon learn and use his special language. The second shock is the astonishing range of specialized, technically-oriented words – starting with buffer, stack, input work queue, console, compiler, software, hardware, data protection, interface, compatibility, bits and bytes – which tend to confuse people at first sight. Again, a simple meaning hides behind most words.

Most people will not actually come face to face with the complex planning and fault-finding (or debugging) involved in making a computer do their task correctly and economically. They will become users, taking advantage of the many excellent training courses offered both by schools and producers. Some worry about the threat of losing their job; yet the computer can eliminate hundreds of extremely boring tasks, enabling the secretary, for example, to compose an individual letter or report, while routine work is handled by the computer. The bank clerk need no longer worry about end-of-month statements, as the computer does this simply and with unfailing accuracy.

The scientist can perform tasks which would literally take a man tens of millions of years to do by hand, while perfect designs of the wind's effects on a car's speed can, for instance, be studied within seconds on a screen, and corrected where necessary. Clearly the computer is creating "thinking" jobs while opening fascinating new careers for many. In Britain all schools will soon have computing science as a compulsory subject, and the BBC TV has been showing a beginner's course for several years, which is watched by so many intrigued viewers that a special computer had to be designed and built for the next series. Sales there are now above half a million!

Evidently we cannot afford to ignore the computer. In fact, the next generation of aircraft will be flown by the pilot speaking to the computer which does the actual flying. Let's leave the last word to "The Times". When a regular weekly feature is devoted to computing, then surely it is here to stay.

aggressive	agressiv, angriffig
universal tool	Universalgerät
unemployment	Arbeitslosigkeit
calculating machine	Rechenmaschine
vast	riesig
countless	zahllos
speed	Schnelligkeit, Tempo
huge	enorm
display screen	Bildschirm
repetitive	(sich)wiederholend
printer	Drucker
print-out	Computerausdruck
simplify, to	erleichtern, vereinfachen
manual	manuell
cross-checking	kontrollieren und gegenkontrollieren
in short supply	knapp werden
optical reader	optischer Lesestift
warning note	Warnzeichen
reorder	nachbestellen
astonishing	erstaunlich
data protection	Datenschutz
tend, to	tendieren, neigen
confuse, to	verwirren, verwechseln
fault-finding	Fehlersuche
debugging	Fehlersuche
economical	ökonomisch, wirtschaftlich

threat	Gefahr, Drohung
eliminate, to	eliminieren, vernichten
enable, to	ermöglichen
compose, to	zusammensetzen, aufsetzen
unfailing	unfehlbar
accuracy	Genauigkeit, Sorgfalt
scientist	Wissenschafter
perform, to	ausführen, verrichten
literally	buchstäblich
effect	Auswirkung
create, to	(er)schaffen
career	Laufbahn
computing science	Computerkunde, Informatik
compulsory	obligatorisch
intrigued	gefesselt, erstaunt
viewer	(Fernseh)zuschauer
design, to	entwerfen, entwickeln
series	(Fernseh)folge
evidently	offenbar, offensichtlich
afford, to	sich leisten
ignore, to	ignorieren, nicht beachten
aircraft	Flugzeug
actual	eigentlich
feature	Spezialartikel, Rubrik
devote, to	widmen

Vocabulary exercise

Choose the correct words from the list
1. Some people seem afraid when ____ are ____.
2. This may be because they ____ it may ____ ____ their work and cause ____.
3. However the computer does ____ work and has ____ new ____ for many people.
4. Information is stored on a ____ medium, almost like that of a cassette tape ____.
5. There are a vast number of ____ functions by which a computer saves ____ and time.
6. The computer will also ____ the stockkeeper on a ____ when to place an ____ for more stock.
7. However instructions must be written in a special ____ like Basic.
8. Users have to know ____ words like console and ____.
9. Bank clerks and secretaries can do ____ work, and leave ____ jobs to the computer.
10. There are many ____ to learn how to ____ this equipment on TV or through ____ courses.

boring
brought
careers
computers
fear
individual
language
mentioned
opportunities
order
recorder
repetitive
routine
screen
show
software
special
take over
tape
training
unemployment
use
work

SELBY CAR ACCESSORIES
2 Barlby Road
Doncaster, DO3 7BC

Mr J. Staindrop
Moorex Computing
38 The Headrow
Leeds
LI2 4EP

22 November 19..

Your Ref JS/Cus/763
Our Ref PB/Sys/BU

Dear Mr Staindrop

Thank you for the recent information on the delivery date of our new computer system and the brochure about your computer science and operating courses. As we now have little more than two months before the changeover to an on-line system we feel it opportune to organize relevant education.

As you certainly know, we shall have to cover the varying needs of the staff in the warehouse, in the offices, and obviously those who actually serve the customers. Therefore, it would seem logical to train those on consoles using visual display units separately from staff dealing with the central processing unit.

Further, we would appreciate the opportunity of training our employees on the other peripherals such as printers and card-punchers, before we start transferring material. This would ensure that everyone is familiar with addresses, data protection, access to data and knows how the programs run.

I should be most grateful if you could let me have a draft training plan by mid-December so that we could fix a date some time in January. Don't hesitate to phone if you require any additional details.

Yours sincerely

Peter Boothby

MOOREX COMPUTING

38 The Headrow   Leeds, L12 4EP

Mr P Boothby
Selby Car Accessories
2 Barlby Road
Doncaster
DO3 7BC   8 December 19..

Your Ref: PB/Sys/BU
Our Ref: JS/Cus/763

Dear Mr Boothby

We are glad to learn from your letter of 22 Nov. 19.. that you would like us to organize the specialist training of your computer staff and employees before your new system is installed. In fact it is a policy of ours always to instruct first on a general basis for a two-day seminar, followed by separate teaching for the various departments.

High up on our list of priorities is familiarization with stops, queries, file maintenance procedures, correct use of optical readers, printers, prompts and displays. These would all be covered extensively in the programme I have arranged for you.

Clearly, there are particular fields like the inventory and warehousing, invoicing and customer records, standing orders and the like which must be thoroughly practised before you go operational. Again, these will be treated in the second phase of the teaching.

I suggest a total of five days' training with the first two-day seminar a fortnight before the second. Possible dates would be the 8/9 January and 22-24 January next.

I hope this outline is what you are looking for, and we would be very pleased to hear the exact numbers of participants so that the computer time can be booked at our training centre.

Yours sincerely

J Staindrop

on-line	direkte Verbindung mit
opportune	vorteilhaft
obviously	selbstverständlich
VDU (visual display unit)	Bildschirmgerät
peripherals	periphere Einheit
ensure, to	gewährleisten
access	Zugriff
CPU (central processing unit)	Zentraleinheit
actually	tatsächlich
stops	Maschinenstop
queries	Frage nach Information
prompts	Rückfrage
file maintenance procedure	Dateiwartung
optical reader	optischer Belegleser
extensively	weitgehend
thoroughly	gründlich
outline	Umriss
feed, to	füttern, eingeben (Daten)
store	Datenspeicher
perfect, to	verbessern

Model Sentences (computers)

1. We are glad to learn from your letter that you are prepared to organize the staff training scheme.
2. We suggest fixing a date in the middle of January.
3. The CPU (Central processing unit) consists of a processor and a main store.
4. Specialised training is required for people working with computers.
5. Most portable-computer manufacturers are trying to perfect their liquid-crystal displays (LCD's).
6. The portable computer has come a long way since the first battery-powered model was introduced.
7. Everyone should be familiar with the routines before operations are started.
8. These aspects of the work on a console will be thoroughly trained during the two-day seminar.
9. Computers are used nowadays for many different kinds of work.
10. The data fed, or put, into a computer is input data.

Sentences for translation

1. Der Gedanke, dass eine Maschine menschliche Arbeit übernehmen könnte, verursacht Unsicherheit und Furcht.
2. Tatsächlich ist der Computer eine äusserst schnelle Rechenmaschine mit einem elektronischen Gedächtnis.
3. Tausende von Fakten können aufgenommen, gespeichert, abgerufen und nach Wunsch verarbeitet werden.

4. Der Benutzer muss die benötigte Spezialsprache und die technische Bedienung verstehen.
5. Gewisse Arbeitsplätze dürften wegrationalisiert [= eliminiert] werden; aber es gibt Aussicht[en] auf kreative Tätigkeiten und Berufe in der Datenverarbeitung.

Letters for translation

Sehr geehrter Herr

Seit einiger Zeit haben wir nun versucht, einen passenden Computerkurs für unsere Belegschaft zu finden. Ihre Firma wurde durch einen Computerfachmann vorgeschlagen.
Was wir gerne fragen würden ist, ob Sie einen Trainingskurs für unsere Büroangestellten organisieren könnten, während dem diese lernen würden, wie man die grundlegenden Elemente des Computergebrauchs anwendet. Wir werden in der Zeit nach Neujahr ein neues Computersystem installieren und würden deshalb einen Termin im frühen Januar begrüssen [= zu schätzen wissen].
Wir wären sehr dankbar, wenn Sie uns ein Angebot auf der Basis von 5 Tagen in Ihrem Trainingscenter für insgesamt 23 Büroangestellte machen könnten.
Bitte zögern Sie nicht, uns wegen weiterer Einzelheiten anzurufen, aber beachten Sie bitte, dass ich in den kommenden vierzehn Tagen wegen einer Händlerausstellung nur morgens verfügbar bin.

Letter writing assignments

Schreiben Sie in Peter Boothbys Namen einen Brief an Moorex, in dem Sie sich mit dem vorgeschlagenen Kursprogramm einverstanden erklären. Bitten Sie aber um eine Verschiebung des zweiten Kurstages. Begründen Sie Ihr Begehren und nennen Sie ein Alternativdatum. Abschliessend teilen Sie der Moorex noch die Art und Anzahl der Teilnehmer mit.

10 The warehouse

A warehouse is a large building where raw materials, or semi-finished products and manufactured goods are stored. In addition incoming deliveries are received at the warehouse, and it is the starting place for consignments that are sent off to distributors, retailers or the consumer.

The parts or goods stored are numbered. A list or index showing the quantity is the inventory. It is usual for a stockkeeper or the warehouse supervisor to take stock at the beginning of each year by checking the inventory with the items actually stored on the warehouse shelves, in racks or drawers.

If the work of a warehouse is to function efficiently, it must be well organized. When goods arrive the stockkeeper unpacks and checks them with the relevant delivery note or invoice before storing them in their appropriate place or sending them to their destination. Then stock records are completed. Card indexes have given way to computer control, so that goods dispatched from the warehouse are recorded instantly. The screen or a print-out shows when stocks of a particular part are getting low and should be re-ordered. Handling, packing and weighing are largely mechanized. The warehouse is close to a good road, an airport, a railway siding, canal, river or seaport for transport to be made as speedily and economically as possible.

raw material	*Rohmaterial*
semi-finished product	*Halbfabrikat*
manufactured goods	*Fertigprodukte*
store, to	*lagern*
in addition	*zusätzlich*
consignment	*Versand*
distributor	*Verteiler, Wiederverkäufer*
index	*Index, Register*
inventory	*Inventar, Lagerbestand*
stockkeeper	*Magaziner, Lagerist*
supervisor	*Kontrolleur, Aufseher*
take stock, to	*Inventur machen*
shelf	*Fach, Regal*
rack	*Gestell*
drawer	*Schublade*
delivery note	*Lieferschein*
appropriate	*angemessen, geeignet*
destination	*Bestimmung(sort), Ziel*
stock records	*Lagerliste, Vorratsliste*
record, to	*aufzeichnen, erfassen*
instantly	*sofort*
screen	*Schirm*
particular	*bestimmte*
get low, to	*Tiefstand erreichen*
re-order, to	*nachbestellen*

handle, to	handhaben, abwickeln
weigh, to	wägen
railway siding	Anschlussgleis
speedy	schnell, zügig
economical	wirtschaftlich
advice note	Versandanzeige
accounting	Buchhaltung

Vocabulary exercise

Choose the correct words from the list.
1 The ____ is the building where ____ products and ____ goods are stored.
2 The customers may be ____, ____ or ____ in various parts of the country.
3 Goods held in the warehouse are ____ in an ____.
4 It is the job of a warehouse ____ or ____ to take ____ once a year.
5 When the stockkeeper unpacks the goods, he has to ____ them with the ____ or ____ received at the same time.
6 Computer ____ is used to ____ stocks.
7 When stocks ____ the relevant parts must be ____.
8 If the warehouse is close to a ____ or seaport, transport can be made ____ and ____.

check
control
consumers
delivery note
distributors
economically
get low
inventory
invoice
listed
manufactured
railway siding
record
re-ordered
retailers
semi-finished
speedily
stock
stockkeeper
supervisor
warehouse

85

THE UNDERSMITH CO (EUROPE) AG

12 Gotthardstrasse
6300 Zug, Switzerland

Undersmith Typewriter Co Inc
Shipping Department
52 Third Avenue
Cleveland, Ohio 44133 USA   August 20, 19..

For the attention of Mr S Harrison

Our order No 0147/B/7

Gentlemen:

We refer to our order of July 4, 19.. and to your consignment dispatched from Cleveland on 30 July. Your advice note covering this consignment includes all the items we ordered. However, on unpacking the two cases marked

    UT
    ASD   Nos 1 and 2
    4

we find that the contents do not tally with the documents. We have received all the typewriters, but the spare parts have not yet arrived.

As we are in urgent need of these parts, we should appreciate prompt delivery of the goods. Please let us know when we may expect them.

                              Very truly yours
                              The Undersmith Co (Europe)

                              Beat Weitner

UNDERSMITH TYPEWRITER CO., INC.
52 THIRD AVENUE, CLEVELAND, OHIO 44133

The Undersmith Co (Europe) AG
12 Gotthardstrasse
6300 Zug
Switzerland

August 27, 19..

Attention: Mr. Beat Weitner

Our consignment of July 30, 19..
(your Order No. 0147/B/7)

Gentlemen:

With reference to your letter notifying us of a short shipment of goods, we trust you have in the meantime received the remainder of the delivery.

The discrepancy was due to the fact that the carriers were not able to accept the full consignment on July 30, and had to leave one case to be collected the following day. In this way it became separated from the other cases, but was, we understand, shipped on the same day by another steamer, ss 'Concordia', unloading at Rotterdam on August 18.

Please, let us know if the second part of this consignment has not arrived; in this case we shall notify our forwarders and insurance company.

Very truly yours
Undersmith Typewriter Co Inc

S. Harrison
Shipping Department

tally with, to	übereinstimmen
cover, to	umfassen
include, to	enthalten
contents	Inhalt
spare parts	Ersatzteile
notify, to	mitteilen, anzeigen
short shipment	Manko
remainder	Rest
discrepancy	Unstimmigkeit
separate, to	(ab)sondern, (aus)scheiden
unload, to	entladen, löschen (Ladung)

Model sentences (inventory/logistic)

1 Although we keep an accurate check of our stocks, a discrepancy is possible.
2 Our stock is low at present, but new supplies are expected next week.
3 The catalogue lists all the items by their part numbers.
4 We can assure you that the quantity was carefully checked when the cases were unpacked.
5 When you place your order, please give us full instructions for packing and delivery.
6 We sent you the advice note on the same date as the goods left our warehouse.
7 The boxes we have received contain only ten springs No 434-01. The packing list shows 16 of these.
8 Our delivery charges are economical, as our warehouse is situated between the motorway and the railway goods siding.
9 We have today dispatched the consignment of office furniture from our Liverpool warehouse, as can be seen from the enclosed advice of dispatch.
10 Since we received no forwarding instructions, we have had to warehouse the goods since 14 May.
11 We are pleased to inform you that the raw materials will be collected on the morning of 8 September, for road transport to Southampton.

Sentences for translation

1. Beim Vergleich der Ware mit der Versandanzeige bemerkten wir, dass 12 Artikel fehlten.
2. Einmal im Jahr wird Inventur gemacht.
3. Wir bestehen darauf, dass Sie die Ersatzteile ohne Verzögerung per Luftpost schicken.
4. Eingehende und ausgehende Waren werden vom Computer erfasst.
5. Der Bildschirm oder ein (Computer-)Ausdruck zeigt, wenn Lager knapp werden.

6. Beim Auspacken der Kisten stellten wir fest, dass der Inhalt nicht mit den Dokumenten übereinstimmt.
7. Die Artikelnummern zeigen an, wo die Waren gelagert sind.
8. Kopien der Versandanzeige werden gemacht, um als Lieferschein, Packliste usw. zu dienen.
9. Diese Sendungen müssen unser Lagerhaus bis spätestens 21. Juni verlassen, da wir den Platz für andere Rohmaterialien benötigen.
10. Die bestellten Waren stehen zu Ihrer Verfügung; bitte geben Sie uns Ihre Verschiffungs- und Versicherungsanweisungen.

Letters for translation

1. Von: Caran d'Ache, 1200 Genf, Schweiz
   An: Mahmoud Ekziel, 17 Seven Sisters Road, Alexandria, Egypt

   15. März 19..

   Wir beziehen uns auf Ihre Bestellung vom 22. Februar für 1000 Gros Bleistifte HB. Diese Ware ist nun versandbereit. Ihre Nachbestellung vom 28. Februar von weiteren 200 Gros kann nächste Woche geliefert werden.
   In Ihrem Auftrag vom 22. Februar informierten Sie uns, dass uns Ihre Spediteure Versandanweisungen geben würden. Wir haben bis jetzt noch nichts von ihnen gehört und werden ihnen darum eine Kopie dieses Briefes schikken.
   Wir hoffen, dass Sie mit der Ausführung dieses Auftrages zufrieden sein werden.

   Mit freundlichen Grüssen

   Kopie an: Firma Guardi & Cie
   Spediteure
   Genua, Italien

2. Sehr geehrter Herr Brandon

   Wir bestätigen den Empfang Ihrer Sendung und Ihrer Rechnung Nr. B/278 vom 19. Oktober.
   Bei der Kontrolle bemerkten wir, dass die gelieferten Waren von einer helleren Farbe als das Muster und infolgedessen weniger zum Verkauf geeignet sind.
   Falls Sie uns einen Rabatt von 20% einräumen, sind wir bereit, die Waren zu behalten. Falls nicht, werden wir die Sendung zurückschicken müssen.

   Mit freundlichen Grüssen

Letter writing assignments

Master Watches, Le Locle, teilt Hutton Wholesalers mit, dass die bestellten Uhren verpackt und gemäss Anweisungen abgeschickt worden sind. Die Versandanweisung liegt dem Brief bei; Verpackungsliste und Lieferschein jedoch befinden sich bei der Sendung. Der Kunde schliesslich wird die Rechnung in der kommenden Woche erhalten.

11 Invoices, statements and cheques

The copy of the advice note which is for the accounts department is the basis for an invoice to be sent to the customer. Normally it is sent as printed matter or second-class mail without a covering letter; on the other hand some companies use this opportunity to write to the customer, thanking him and paving the way to further business. Where credit has not yet been allowed, for instance to a new customer, a pro forma invoice is submitted, asking for payment before the goods can be dispatched, or goods for a smaller order may be supplied on COD terms (cash on delivery).

At the end of the month or quarter each customer receives a statement of account, listing the transactions during the period and indicating the balance outstanding. On the Continent the most common methods of payment are the bank transfer or the postal giro system. In England and America post offices do not usually deal with the transfer of money to any extent. Most payments are made by bank cheques. Not only business firms, but most private individuals have an account with a bank, a current account (Am. checking account). They can pay money into this account, have cheques (checks) booked to their credit, and they can make payments by cheque, on condition that there is enough money on deposit to cover the cheque.

The payer simply fills in and signs the cheque, mails it to the payee, who endoreses it by signing his name on the back. He then passes it on to his bank for the amount to be put to his credit. Crossing a cheque, so that payment may only be made to the recipient's account, ensures that no misuse can be made, even if it goes astray in the mail (Am. check with restrictive endorsement). These cheques are not negotiable, that means they cannot be transferred to someone else's account by endorsement. Other cheques, like bearer cheques and travellers checks, can be cashed over any bank counter.

statement (of account) S/A	Kontoauszug
printed matter	Drucksache
covering letter	Begleitbrief
pave the way, to	den Weg bahnen
quarter	Quartal
indicate, to	angeben, anzeigen
balance	Saldo
outstanding	ausstehend
transfer	Überweisung
current account	Kontokorrent
checking account (US)	Kontokorrent
on deposit	in der Einlage
payee	Zahlungsempfänger
endorse, to	indossieren
crossed cheque	gekreuzter Check, Verrechnungscheck
cheque with restrictive endorsement	gekreuzter Check, Verrechnungscheck

recipient		*Empfänger*
misuse		*Missbrauch*
go astray, to		*in die Irre gehen, hier: abhanden kommen*
negotiable		*verkehrsfähig*
bearer cheque		*Inhabercheck*
cash, to		*einlösen*

---

seit — since: from a certain point in the past
for: a length of time until the present
(also *für, während*)

Mr Secrest has been with us since the end of last month; he has been working here for a fortnight.

Vocabulary exercise

Choose the correct words from the list.

1 The invoice is based on the ___ which has come from the ___.
2 Suppliers sometimes write a ___ letter to ___ the way to further business.
3 A new customer for whom credit ___ have not yet been arranged, receives a ___ invoice.
4 If the order is small, goods are conveniently sent ___.
5 A ___ of account shows the ___ of the month or quarter and the ___ outstanding.
6 Businessmen in Britain and the USA generally use banks for the ___ of money.
7 Firms normally have a ___ account with a bank.
8 A crossed cheque is not ___; it may only be ___ to the ___ account.
9 A check with ___ endorsement cannot be misused, if it goes ___.
10 You can easily cash a ___ cheque at a bank ___.

advice note
astray
balance
bearer
COD
counter
covering
credited
current
negotiable
pave
payee's
pro forma
restrictive
statement
terms
transactions
transfer
warehouse

THE UNDERSMITH CO (EUROPE) AG

12 Gotthardstrasse
6300 Zug, Switzerland

Messrs Mulder en Ruig
Lange Kerkstraat 80
4461 JK Goes, Netherlands   3 August 19..

Dear Sirs

We were very pleased to receive your order of 1 August for machines and parts to the value of Dfl 2,800. As this is your first order with us and you require early delivery, would you please remit your cheque against the Pro Forma Invoice enclosed herewith.

The goods you require are available for you, and we shall dispatch them immediately on receipt of your payment. For future business we shall of course be pleased to grant you credit facilities, and for this purpose we should appreciate receiving the names of firms or a bank as your references.

We look forward to doing further business with you in the future.

                                        Yours faithfully

Enclosure

THE UNDERSMITH CO (EUROPE) AG
12 Gotthardstrasse
6300 Zug, Switzerland

Messrs R Bender & Co
Freiestrasse 34
4002 Basel

August 3, 19..

Dear Sirs,

It was a pleasure to receive your Order No DS 116 of July 27. The printers were sent to your address yesterday, as can be seen from the enclosed invoice.

We trust they will reach you in perfect condition and that this order will lead to your placing another order with us when you need equipment again.

Very truly yours

R Fischer
Sales Department

Model sentences (invoices and payments)

1. We have pleasure in sending you enclosed our invoice in duplicate for goods amounting to £ 340.
2. As arranged we enclose our statement for transactions up to 30 June.
3. Would you kindly let us have your remittance before the end of this month.
4. Will you please send us a cheque against the pro forma invoice attached.
5. In payment of your pro forma invoice we enclose a cheque for £ 1,700.
6. At today's rate of exchange this is equivalent to Sfr. ...
7. In settlement of your account we enclose a sight draft.
8. We have instructed the ... Bank to transfer the amount of your invoice to your account No. ...
9. Our bank will make a SWIFT transfer* of the amount outstanding to your bank account.
10. We were pleased to receive your check for $ 2,640. It has been credited to your account, which is now completely clear.
11. We cannot, unfortunately, grant you the discount you deducted from the invoice amount. Please send us a remittance for the balance of ...
12. Our quarterly statement is enclosed. If payment is made by the end of the month 2% discount may be deducted.

* SWIFT Society for Worldwide Interbank Financial Telecommunication

Sentences for translation

1. Hiermit senden wir Ihnen unsere Rechnung über den Betrag von £ 39 für die Waren, die wir Ihnen am 20. März gesandt haben.
2. Beiliegend finden Sie Ihren Kontoauszug für den Monat Juli.
3. Wollen Sie bitte den Auszug kontrollieren und uns den ausstehenden Betrag im Laufe der nächsten Woche überweisen.
4. Wir danken Ihnen für Ihre Bestellung vom 11. Oktober, für die die Pro Forma-Rechnung beigefügt ist.
5. Da dies eine Erstbestellung ist, werden wir die Waren «bar bei Lieferung» zustellen.
6. Wir haben gestern Ihre Maschinen in gutem Zustand erhalten.
7. Wir haben unsere Bank angewiesen, den Rechnungsbetrag an Ihre Bank in Manchester zu überweisen.
8. Wir haben den Kontoauszug per 31. Juli geprüft und für richtig befunden.
9. Wir legen einen Check über den Saldo von £ 235 bei.
10. Zum Ausgleich Ihres Kontos legen wir einen Sichtwechsel bei.

Letters for translation

Von: The Hutton Wholesalers Ltd, 125 King William Street, London EC4 3PJ
An: Master Watches SA, 2400 Le Locle, Schweiz

Unsere Ref: PS: lt
Ihre Ref: FW: JD 4. April 19..

Sehr geehrte Herren

Wir danken Ihnen für Ihren Brief vom 28. März 19.. und die umgehende Lieferung des Mod. 05. Die Uhren sind hier am Montag in gutem Zustand angekommen.
Zum Ausgleich [= Bezahlung] Ihrer Rechnung legen wir einen Scheck über £ 863.50 bei, was – zu augenblicklichen Wechselkursen – dem Gegenwert von Sfr. 2665.– entspricht.
Wir freuen uns, mit Ihnen weitere Geschäfte zu tätigen, sobald wir wieder Armbanduhren benötigen.

Mit freundlichen Grüssen

Letter writing assignments

Schreiben Sie einen Brief im Namen von Bender & Co, Freiestrasse 34, 4002 Basel, datiert vom 1. September 19...
Danken Sie Undersmith (Europe) für die schnelle Lieferung der Drucker und legen Sie einen gekreuzten Check zur Deckung der Rechnung vom 3. August 19.. über Sfr. 4027.– (Rechnungsbetrag abzüglich 2% Skonto) bei. Sollten die neuen Geräte zufriedenstellend arbeiten, werden wohl in nächster Zukunft noch einige Schreibmaschinen durch Drucker ausgetauscht.

12 Reminders and part payments

In spite of references for credit rating which have been obtained in reply to status inquiries (Ch 8), customers with credit accounts sometimes delay in settling their debts. They may have encountered a period of bad business, and if they write to the creditors an extension may be given for part of the payment.

In other cases when a customer fails to make payment, the seller must remind him of the due date. In a first reminder he assumes that the matter has been overlooked. He brings it to the customer's attention by means of a copy invoice or statement. A humorous letter can have an advantage in the early stages of collection. If this has no effect it is followed by another collection letter, expressing in stronger terms that payment must be made by a given date, and that interest is due on the outstanding balance. A final notice, in the form of a registered letter, warns the debtor of more serious consequences which will involve him in extra expenses, for instance referring the matter to a collection agency or a lawyer.

reminder	Mahnung
credit rating	Kreditwürdigkeit
collection letter	Mahnbrief
delay, to	aufschieben, verzögern
settle a debt, to	Schuld begleichen
extension	Verlängerung
fail, to	unterlassen, versäumen
due date	Verfalldatum
overlook, to	übersehen
advantage	Vorteil
interest	Zins
due	fällig
notice	Meldung, Mitteilung
registered	eingeschrieben
warn of, to	warnen vor
debtor	Schuldner
collection agency	Inkassobüro

Vocabulary exercise

Choose the correct words from the list.
1 Favourable ____ may have been received, but some customers nevertheless ____ in paying their ____.
2 An ____ can be allowed if a customer has ____ bad business.
3 However there are other cases when customers ____ to make ____.
4 Then the creditor sends a ____ to point out that payment is ____, enclosing a copy of the ____.

collection
collection agency
creditor
debtor
debts
delay
due
encountered
expenses

97

5   Still another ____ letter may have to be written.
6   Extra ____ for the debtor are involved for ____ on the ____ balance, or legal costs.
7   If, after several reminders, the ____ does not pay, the ____ sends a ____ letter.
8   He may refer the matter to a ____ or a ____.

extension
fail
interest
lawyer
outstanding
payment
references
registered
reminder
statement

---

15 October 19..

Dear Sir

May we draw your attention to the enclosed copy of our statement made up to 30 September 19.. showing a balance in our favour of £ 250.

No doubt, it is through an oversight on your part that settlement is now two weeks overdue, and we look forward to receiving your remittance within the next few days.

Yours faithfully

Enc

---

31 October 19..

Dear Sir

On 30 September 19.. we sent you our statement, showing an outstanding balance of £ 250. As we did not receive your cheque in payment of the account, we reminded you of the matter on 15 October, enclosing a duplicate statement, to which we asked you to give your early attention.

According to the conditions of sale, your remittance was due on 30 September 19.., more than four weeks ago. Please send us your cheque by 6 November 19..

Yours faithfully

Enc

THE UNDERSMITH CO (EUROPE) AG
12 Gotthardstrasse
6300 Zug, Switzerland

REGISTERED

6 November 19..

Dear Sirs

Our S/A dated 30 September 19..

It surprises us that we have not had a reply to our repeated requests for payment. As we are unable to keep this balance of £250 open any longer, we must insist on receiving payment by 10 November 19.. Failing this we shall be compelled to take legal action to recover the debt.

We also reserve the right to charge you 6% interest on arrears as from 30 September 19.., the date on which settlement became due.

Yours faithfully

International Traders Inc.

56 Central Street
Seattle 98122

The State Suppliers Inc.
419 West Street
Houston, Texas 83192

May 10, 19..

Gentlemen:

We refer to your invoice COU-905 dated April 2, and have the pleasure in enclosing our check for $840 as part payment.

Due to poor weather conditions business was slack, and our turnover in deck chairs proved to be very disappointing. This setback has put us in some difficulty; we have a large number left on our hands, but hope to dispose of them now that the summer season is approaching.

Would you allow us to postpone settlement of the rest of your account? We thank you in advance for your understanding.

Very truly yours

INTERNATIONAL TRADERS INC.

Enc

THE STATE SUPPLIERS INC.
419 West Street   Houston, Texas 83192

International Traders Inc.
56 Central Street
Seattle, Washington 98122

May 13, 19..

Gentlemen:

Thank you for your check for $840, which we have accepted as payment on account. After careful consideration of your letter of May 10 we have decided to allow you additional time in which to pay the balance of your overdue account.

In difficult times exceptions can be made to our general credit terms. In return for this favour we are sure that you will meet your liabilities when payment becomes due.

We look forward to receiving the sum of $760 by June 10, which represents a further one month's postponement.

Very truly yours

STATE SUPPLIERS INCORPORATED
Credit Department

```
    DEAR FRIEND -

        The best of business friends may part,
        Although it often breaks a heart.
            We wrote to you a month ago,
            And wrote again - as you may know.
                A pound or two's not much to pay,
                So won't you send your cheque today?
                    It would be sad to lose your trade
                    So we are hoping you have paid.

                    CREDIT DEPARTMENT
```

in our favour	zu unseren Gunsten
oversight	Versehen
overdue	überfällig
S/A, statement of account	Kontoübersicht
register (a letter), to	einschreiben
insist on, to	bestehen auf
compel, to	zwingen, nötigen
take legal action, to	Rechtsweg beschreiten
recover, to	wieder einbringen, einziehen
reserve the right, to	Recht vorbehalten
arrears	Rückstände, Schulden
slack	flau, lustlos
setback	Rückschlag
dispose of, to	veräussern
postpone, to	aufschieben
payment on account	Teilzahlung
consideration	Erwägung, Überlegung
commitment	Verpflichtung
hardly	kaum

Model sentences (reminders and part payments)

1. Our statement of 29 April appears to have escaped your notice.
2. May we remind you that your remittance was due on 31 December.
3. It is no doubt through an oversight that settlement of our invoice has not yet been made.
4. If your cheque is on the way, please accept our best thanks and disregard this reminder.
5. Please let us know if there is any reason for this non-payment.
6. We cannot keep this account open any longer.
7. This is our final request for payment.

8   As we have not yet received a remittance, in spite of repeated reminders, we shall reluctantly be compelled to take legal steps.
9   We shall instruct our solicitor (Am. attorney) to institute legal proceedings.
10 We should be very grateful to you if we may pay the outstanding amount in monthly instalments.
11 Your concession will enable us to clear the balance within the next quarter.
12 As you have always paid your accounts promptly so far, we are prepared to grant you the extension asked for.
13 Although we understand your difficulties, we cannot allow you to postpone payment any longer.

erinnern	to remember	*sich erinnern an, grüssen, nicht vergessen*
	I remembered the fact.	
	Remember me to Mr. Sigrist.	
	Remember to call on us when you are in London.	
	to remind someone	*jemand erinnern an, mahnen*
	Please remind me to phone them.	
	We have reminded them of the matter several times.	

Sentences for translation

1. Wir sind bereit, Ihnen einen Zahlungsaufschub von höchstens 30 Tagen zu gewähren.
2. Wir bedauern, dass es (für Sie) nötig war, uns an das Verfalldatum der Rechnung zu erinnern.
3. Wir werden der Angelegenheit unverzüglich nachgehen [= untersuchen]; der fällige Betrag wird Ihnen so bald als möglich überwiesen.
4. Wir legen einen Kontoauszug mit Stand Ende Juni bei, der einen Saldo zu unsern Gunsten von Sfr. 920.– zeigt.
5. Da die Zahlung nun seit vier Wochen überfällig ist, sehen wir dem Erhalt Ihrer Überweisung innert 10 Tagen entgegen.
6. Falls Ihre Zahlung nicht bis zum 11. Februar eintrifft, sehen wir uns genötigt, 6% Zins auf dem ausstehenden Betrag zu belasten.
7. Unter diesen Umständen hoffen wir, dass Sie uns erlauben, die Bezahlung des Restbetrages aufzuschieben.
8. Wir können Ihnen versichern, dass wir unseren Verpflichtungen innert dreier Monate nachkommen werden.
9. Obwohl wir normalerweise keinen Aufschub [= Verlängerung] gewähren, wollen wir in diesem Fall Ihrem Vorschlag zustimmen.
10. Wir sind nicht in der Lage, weitere Ausnahmen zu machen, und müssen nun den Rechtsweg beschreiten, um die Schuld einzuziehen.

Letters for translation

1. Von: Undersmith Co (Europe) AG, 12 Gotthardstrasse, 6300 Zug
   An: Electra Holding Corp., Gubelstrasse 12, 1203 Genf

   20. September 19..

   Dürfen wir Sie daran erinnern, dass wir Ihnen am 31. Juli einen Kontoauszug gesandt haben. Der Betrag von Fr. 9349.80 war am 31. August fällig.
   Wir schätzen die Pünktlichkeit sehr, mit der Sie Ihren bisherigen Verpflichtungen nachgekommen sind. Können Sie uns den Grund mitteilen, warum Sie dieses Mal die Zahlung hinausgeschoben haben? Wenn es sich als notwendig erweisen sollte, wären wir bereit, Ihnen Zahlungserleichterungen zu gewähren. Jedoch müssen wir Sie bitten, uns bis Ende September dieses Jahres einen beträchtlichen Teil des ausstehenden Betrages zu überweisen.

   Mit freundlichen Grüssen

2. Von: Electra Holding Corp., Gubelstrasse 12, 1203 Genf
   An: Undersmith Co (Europe) AG, 12 Gotthardstrasse, 6300 Zug

   29. September 19..

   Ihr Kontoauszug vom 31. Juli: Fr. 9349.80

   Es tut uns sehr leid, dass Sie uns an den fälligen Betrag erinnern mussten. Wir hätten unseren Verpflichtungen rechtzeitig nachkommen können, wenn uns ein bedeutender Kunde nicht im Stich gelassen hätte. Daher sind wir für Ihren Vorschlag dankbar und schicken Ihnen als Teilzahlung einen Scheck über Fr. 3000.–. Wir sind sicher, Ihnen den Rest des Betrages bis Ende Oktober überweisen zu können.

   Mit freundlichen Grüssen

   Beilage: Scheck

Letter writing assignments

Sie haben bereits einmal einen amerikanischen Kunden aufgefordert, seine offenstehende Rechnung zu begleichen – vergebens.
Schreiben Sie eine zweite Mahnung in einem etwas entschlosseneren Ton.

13 Processing orders

When a supplier receives an order from an agent or a customer, he enters or books it, and sends an order acknowledgement — a letter or a printed form. This is to thank the customer and inform him of the date on which delivery will be made. At the same time it is the seller's formal acceptance of the order. The copies provide the necessary instructions for dispatch as well as records of the order.

Occasionally a supplier cannot process an order as it stands. Some customers may have an old price-list, quoting a lower price for the merchandise than that currently applicable. Occasionally stocks of certain items have to be replenished, and the articles or parts cannot be delivered within the time required. Wherever possible the supplier will offer a substitute for goods that cannot be provided, rather than refuse an order.

Buyers do not always accept the prices and terms quoted by the seller unconditionally, and may make a counter-proposal in order to obtain more favourable prices, or a shorter time of delivery. As a result the supplier could make a concession if the customer purchases a large quantity, or especially for an introductory sale.

process, to	verarbeiten
enter, to	hier: buchen
acknowledgement	Bestätigung
provide, to	versehen, versorgen
occasionally	gelegentlich
currently	zur Zeit
applicable	anwendbar
unconditionally	bedingungslos
counter-proposal	Gegenvorschlag
purchase	kaufen, anschaffen

	to confirm	Text/Zeitpunkt bestätigen
bestätigen	we confirm our telegram sent today.	
	Please confirm your verbal instructions.	
	to acknowledge	Empfang bestätigen
	We acknowledge receipt of your letter.	
	The order acknowledgement is enclosed.	

Vocabulary exercise

Choose the correct words from the list.
1 The details of an order received from a customer are ____ or ____ by the supplier.
2 Then he sends an ____, which also serves as an ____ of the order.
3 Copies of the acknowledgement ____ instructions for delivery and are used as ____ of the order.
4 An order cannot always be ____ on the terms quoted by the customer.
5 There may have been an ____ in price or stock may have to be ____.
6 When articles are not ____ a longer time of ____ is needed.
7 It is better for the supplier to offer a ____ than to ____ the order.
8 Buyers sometimes want to ____ the goods at lower prices and make a ____.
9 The seller occasionally makes a ____ for a large order or an ____ sale.

acceptance
acknowledgement
booked
concession
counter-proposal
delivery
entered
increase
in stock
introductory
processed
provide
purchase
records
refuse
replenished
substitute

THE UNDERSMITH CO (EUROPE) AG
12 Gotthardstrasse
6300 Zug, Switzerland

London School of Business Studies
14 Russell Square
London WC1 "X3   5 July 19..

Attention: Mr K Henderson BA, Director

Dear Sirs

Word Processor U 5002

We have today booked your order of 2 July 19.. for delivery on 20 August.

1 U 2005 flexible disk word processor as ordered, complete with screen, keyboard, printer, with 200 floppy disks, and 100 boxes of ribbon cassettes. Software package UTV for programmed correspondence.

Total price Sfr. 35,000

Terms of payment: Net 60 days, payment
                  by bank cheque of L/C.
Price includes delivery to your school, installation by technicians from our London branch, two days of instruction in September or October and guarantee for repair and full maintenance for 6 months from delivery date.

Mr. John Mason, of our London service department, will contact you by the time you receive the equipment, in order to arrange suitable dates for installation and instruction of your staff. Alternatively, you can reach him by phoning 01-632 47 18.

Thank you for your confidence in our products. You may rely on them and on our best service at all times.

                              Yours faithfully
                              THE UNDERSMITH CO (EUROPE) AG

cc: Undersmith London

Walkwell Footwear plc Northampton N19 3AF
35 Wellington Square England

Snowsport Shoe Company
5000 Aarau
Switzerland

2 October 19..

Dear Sirs

We are obliged to you for your order No G 780 of September 30.

Unfortunately, we cannot supply the MAGNET walking shoes in all the sizes you require, as some these (sizes 6, 7 1/2 and 8) are sold out. As a substitute we can offer you our SUPER walking shoes, which have become extremely popular in this country. From the illustrated leaflet attached you will be able to see that they are only slightly more expensive than the MAGNET brand, and they are more modern in appearance. Moreover these shoes are rather light in weight without being less durable.

As our factory will be producing them all the year round, we can guarantee that sufficient shoes will be available to fill your order. If, under the circumstances, you should prefer to cancel your order for MAGNET shoes, and order the SUPER walking shoes instead, we can deliver the latter ex warehouse. On the other hand, we could supply the MAGNET shoes in the sizes available and SUPER in the missing sizes on request.

May we assure you of our best attention at all times.

Yours faithfully

Enc: Leaflet

R. de Zwarte

Rozemanstraat 22
3023 TS Rotterdam
Nederland

Messrs Sears, Thornton & Co
Rhodes Square
Harare, Zimbabwe   February 25, 19..

<u>Your order d/d Feb 22 for Pencils</u>

Gentlemen:

We have dispatched the undermentioned goods to you today,
following the instructions of your forwarding agents,
Messrs Zwarthout & Co of Rotterdam.

<u>Qty</u>	<u>Description</u>	<u>Packages</u>	<u>Weight</u>
1000 gross (Boxes of 120 tins x 1 doz)	HB Pencils	12 cases	12 cwt 20 lb

<u>Value</u>	<u>Delivery</u>	<u>Marks & Numbers</u>
Dfl 10,800	fob Rotterdam	RZ 1 - 12 SALS

<u>Shipment</u>

By SS FJORDSAIL
Norwegian Maritime Lines

When we receive the Bs/L (bills of lading) from the shipowners,
we shall send you copies together with our insurance policy and
invoice in duplicate.

                                             Very truly yours

                                             Export Department

Copy to: Messrs Zwarthout & Co
             Rotterdam

purchase, to	kaufen, anschaffen
size	Grösse
extremely	ausserordentlich
slightly	ein wenig
expensive	teuer
brand	Marke, Sorte
appearance	Aussehen
durable	dauerhaft, robust
package	Verpackung, Paket
policy	Police

Model sentences (order processing)

1. Thank you for your order of 19 April for typewriter ribbons.
2. You may rely on our carrying out your order promptly in accordance with your instructions.
3. Delivery will be made by 24 October, as requested.
4. We should like to execute the order immediately and send you the goods this week, but must draw your attention to a change in price.
5. You have probably placed your order on the basis of last year's prices; our current price-list is enclosed.
6. As prices are expected to rise again soon, it would be in your own interests to place an order without delay.
7. There has been such a demand for these bags that they are temporarily out of stock.
8. The goods are ready for dispatch now: would you please let us have your delivery instructions.
9. We have recently had several complaints about these tools, and have withdrawn them from production. Please refer to our 19.. catalogue for the present range.
10. We suggest as a subsitute No 820, of which we enclose a sample.
11. This product can be supplied from stock in the quantity you ordered.
12. We hope the goods will reach you in good condition, and look forward to serving you again soon.

Sentences for translation

1. Danke für Ihre Bestellung Nr. A-330, die unsere vollste [= beste] Aufmerksamkeit erhalten wird.
2. Wie Sie aus (dem) beiliegenden Katalog dieses Jahres entnehmen können, werden die von Ihnen bestellten Kunststoffe nicht mehr [länger] hergestellt.
3. Wir senden Ihnen Proben eines verbesserten Ersatzprodukts mit separater Post.
4. Sollten Sie ein billigeres Modell vorziehen, dürfen wir Nr. 1760 vorschlagen, das ebenfalls in zwei Farben erhältlich ist.

5. Bitte teilen Sie uns Ihre Wahl mit, und wir werden Ihre Bestellung zügig ausführen.
6. Da Sie die Waren so dringend benötigen, haben wir sie per Express [Post] gesandt.
7. Es tut uns leid, Sie über eine unerwartete Verzögerung in der Verarbeitung Ihrer Bestellung zu informieren.
8. Wir bestätigen, dass die Spielsachen jetzt per Luftfracht versandt werden, damit sie Sie noch rechtzeitig zum Weihnachtsverkauf erreichen.
9. Unser Lager bearbeitet heute Ihre Bestellung, und wir werden Sie mittels Versandanzeige wissen lassen, wann Sie die Sendung erreichen wird.
10. Falls Sie wünschen, die Waren per Luftfracht zu erhalten, werden wir Ihnen die Zusatzkosten belasten müssen.

Letters for translation

1. Von: Johnson & Co Ltd, Maschinenfabrik, Sheffield SM5 2CF
   An: H. Müller AG, Papierfabrik, Bielefeld, Deutschland
   17. April 19..

   Ihre Bestellung vom 16. April 19.. von zwei Papiermaschinen

   Wir danken für Ihren gestrigen Auftrag, dem wir alle Aufmerksamkeit schenken werden.
   Leider müssen wir Sie darauf aufmerksam machen, dass wir eine Lieferfrist von drei Monaten benötigen. Unsere Maschinen erfreuen sich einer so grossen Nachfrage, dass die Verspätung unvermeidlich geworden ist.
   Sie können sich jedoch auf uns verlassen, dass wir die Papiermaschinen pünktlich in drei Monaten abliefern werden; die hervorragende Qualität wird Sie sicher für die Verzögerung entschädigen.

   Mit freundlichen Grüssen

2. Sehr geehrte Herren

   Wir haben Ihr Schreiben vom 18. dieses Monats erhalten, für das wir Ihnen danken.
   Leider müssen wir Ihnen aber mitteilen, dass wir gezwungen sind, die Preise für unsere Mofas um £ 10 zu erhöhen, da einige Rohstoffe gegenwärtig sehr knapp sind.
   Sobald wir die Bestätigung Ihrer Bestellung erhalten haben, werden wir Sie wissen lassen, wann die Motorfahrräder spediert werden.

   Mit freundlichen Grüssen

Letter writing assignments

1. Lightson Lighters SA, Genf, schreiben an The Madison Stores, 319 Fifth Avenue, New York, wegen der Bestellung von 200 Dutzend Feuerzeugen. Das Genfer Unternehmen bedankt sich und teilt mit, dass das Modell Nr. 112 sofort geliefert werden könne. Nr. 115 hingegen sei erst in etwa zwei Wochen wieder verfügbar. Falls Madison Stores dieses Feuerzeug jedoch früher benötige, schlägt Lightson den Bezug des Modells Nr. 120 vor, das in Qualität und Preis nur unwesentlich von Nr. 115 abweicht und sich in Europa auch ausgezeichnet verkauft. Ein Muster des Modells Nr. 120 wird mit separater Post zugestellt.

   The Madison Stores wird aufgefordert, Lightson so bald als möglich über den Entscheid zu informieren und Lieferanweisungen zuzusenden.

2. Undersmith bestätigt den Empfang der Bestellung von George Thompson & Cie, Office Supplies, 34 avenue Vinet, 1000 Lausanne, vom 8. März. Alle gewünschten Teile sind an Lager, mit Ausnahme des bestellten Software-Pakets. Dieses ist noch in Vorbereitung und wird erst in drei Wochen verfügbar. Der Rest der Bestellung wird – wie in der beiliegenden Bestätigung erwähnt – bis 20. März versandt.

   Undersmith hofft, dass die Software-Verzögerung keine Unannehmlichkeiten bereitet, und dass die Firma auch in Zukunft zu Diensten sein kann.

14 Packing

In sending goods to another address, and especially when shipping them abroad, packing is of important consideration. The final price of goods is influenced by carriage and freight charges, and these are based on the weight or volume of the consignment. In any case goods must arrive at their destination in good condition, and in consideration of this fact the packing used serves to protect them from damage in transit. For this purpose packing materials should be strong and light, and sometimes watertight.

To facilitate handling and loading, bales and cases are frequently stacked onto pallets, or a pallet is attached to the case. There are many types of containers, as illustrated, and some more which are specially made for the articles they contain (eg large machines).

Consumer goods should look attractive to customers in the shops, but this kind of packing is usually referred to as 'packaging'.

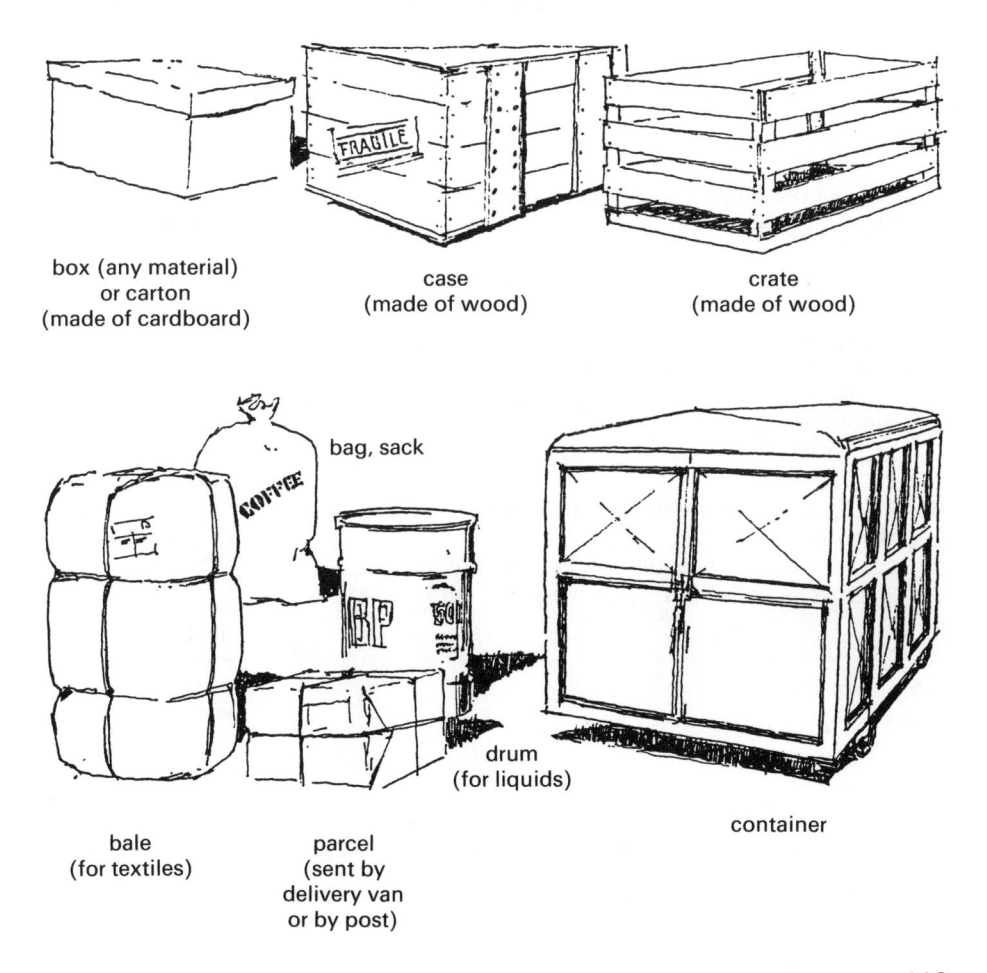

box (any material)
or carton
(made of cardboard)

case
(made of wood)

crate
(made of wood)

bag, sack

bale
(for textiles)

parcel
(sent by
delivery van
or by post)

drum
(for liquids)

container

packing	Verpackung
of consideration	von Belang
influence, to	beeinflussen
base, to	basieren
protect from, to	schützen vor
damage	Schaden
watertight (cases)	wasserdicht
waterproof (paper)	wasserdicht
stack, to	stapeln
pallet	Palette
carton	Pappschachtel
cardboard	Pappe, Kartonpapier
fragile	zerbrechlich
crate	Harrass, Lattenkiste
bale	Ballen
bag, sack	Sack
parcel	Paket
van	Lastwagen, Lieferwagen
drum	Trommel
liquid	flüssig

Vocabulary exercise

Choose the correct words from the list.
1 When goods are shipped ____, ____ is of important ____.
2 Carriage and ____ charges depend among other things on the ____ and volume of the ____.
3 Good packing ____ the contents from damage in ____, because they must reach their ____ in good ____.
4 As sea water may ____ the goods, the packing cases should be ____.
5 ____ differs from packing and is designed to appeal to ____ in shops.
6 A ____ is always made of cardboard and ____ are made of wood.
7 ____ are used for textiles and drums are for ____.
8 ____ are usually sent by delivery ____ or by post.

abroad
bales
carton
condition
consideration
consignment
consumers
crates
damage
destination
freight
liquids
packaging
packing
parcels
protects
transit
van
watertight
weight

TIBERIO & SONS S. P. A.
Via A. Dipieto 3
Turin/ITALIA

The Birmingham Tool Co
24 Snow Street
Birmingham BIR OAA   13 December 19..

Dear Sirs

Our Order No 955 of 29.11

We refer to our recent order for steel spanners, now due for shipment. In order to ensure their arrival here in good condition, would you please observe our packing instructions detailed below.

The spanners should be wrapped separately in oiled paper and packed in strong wooden pallet cases with waterproof lining. To facilitate handling in transit the dimensions should not exceed 3'6" x 2' x 2'.

As the contents will be examined at the customs the lids should be easy to open and fasten. For this purpose, please, airmail to us direct a copy of the packing lists which are included in each case, together with duplicates of the commercial invoice and certificate of origin.

A consignment we recently received from another British firm arrived partly damaged by sea water, resulting in a decrease in value. We would, therefore, urge you to pay particular attention to the packing of this initial order.

                                            Yours faithfully

                                            TIBERIO & SONS S.p.A.
                                            Buying Office

FREEZE-O-CREAM PRODUCTS
Yeoril, Somerset

Cass Packaging Co
125 Edgware Street
London NW6 8RG

3 November 19..

Dear Sirs

We visited your stand at the recent packaging exhibition in London and were very much impressed by the wide selection of packaging manufactured by your company. Our firm produces ice-cream in large quantities and sells on a national scale. In order to maintain our leading position we believe it is necessary to adopt a new display packaging carton similar to the special frozen food wrapping we saw on your stand.

We were given to understand that this packaging contains a non-stick coating which would be ideal for our large size ice-cream packs, provided it can be handled by our present machinery without extensive retooling.

Would you please supply us with full information and a sufficient quantity of cartons to enable us to carry out tests on our equipment.

We hope to hear from you shortly.

                                                Yours faithfully

wrap, to	*einwickeln*
lining	*Auskleidung, Futter*
facilitate, to	*erleichtern*
handle, to	*hantieren, handhaben*
dimension	*Abmessung, Mass*
customs	*Zoll*
lid	*Deckel*
certificate of origin	*Ursprungsbescheinigung, Ursprungszeugnis*
adopt, to	*übernehmen, einführen*
non-stick coating	*nicht-haftender Belag*
provided	*vorausgesetzt*
retooling	*Umrüsten*
equipment	*Ausstattung, Maschinen*

Model sentences (packing)

1. The chemicals are supplied in steel drums of 10 litres.
2. Packing in strong cases with waterproof lining is essential.
3. For transport by air we will use light styrofoam packing.
4. The empties are returnable, freight prepaid, to our warehouse.
5. If not returned, packing will be charged at £ 3.50 per drum.
6. An amount of $ 25 will be credited to you if you return the empty pallet cases.
7. Would you please pack the textiles in bales not exceeding 2 m in length and 3.50 m in girth.
8. Please limit the weight of each box to 20 kg, for convenient stacking on pallets.
9. The packing is to be marked both FRAGILE and THIS SIDE UP, and the cases are to be numbered consecutively.
10. A lighter reinforced type of packing would be more suitable for your needs and can easily be loaded into containers.
11. The coffee is transported in jute bags with a capacity of 100 kg each, impregnated and sealed to conserve the flavour.
12. You have notified us of the weight, but could you also tell us whether your shipment will be a full or a less than full container load?
(full container load = fcl; less than full container load = lcl)

Sentences for translation

1. Wir haben die Waren sehr vorsichtig in wasserdichte Behälter verpackt und hoffen, dass sie in einwandfreiem Zustand ankommen werden.
2. Die vier Maschinen wurden in Kisten verpackt und nach London zur Verschiffung weitergeleitet. Versandanzeige und -papiere sind unterdessen an Sie geschickt worden.
3. Das Nettogewicht der Maschinen beträgt 120 kg, das Bruttogewicht 135 kg.
4. Danke für Ihren Vorschlag, die Teile in starke, mit wasserdichtem Papier

ausgeschlagenen Kisten zu verpacken. Unsere Spediteure werden sich zu Selbstkosten für uns darum kümmern.
5. Um die Handhabung beim Transport zu erleichtern, sollte das Gewicht 50 kg nicht überschreiten.
6. Wir bitten Sie unsere Verpackungsanweisungen zu beachten, deren Einzelheiten auf dem beigefügten Blatt angegeben sind.
7. Die Harrasse, die wir für Exportaufträge verwenden, sind mit «zerbrechlich» bezeichnet und für diesen Zweck sehr geeignet.
8. Unsere Firma kann Ihnen ein breites Sortiment an Verpackungsarten in verschiedenen Materialien anbieten.
9. Die Textilien werden in Ballen verpackt, in wasserfestes Material eingewikkelt und mit Metallbändern verschlossen werden.
10. Die beiliegende Rechnung weist eine Belastung von 7 Dollar für jede der von Ihnen behaltenen Trommeln auf.

Letters for translation

Von: Schröter & Müller AG, Maschinen und Werkzeuge, Industriestrasse 8, 9010 St. Gallen
An: The Birmingham Tool Company, 224 Snow Street, Birmingham BIR 0AA

8. Januar 19..

Ihre Firma wurde uns von unseren Geschäftsfreunden Tiberio & Söhne in Turin empfohlen.
Wir benötigen regelmässig Werkzeuge und könnten sie von Ihnen kaufen. Wir möchten aber schon jetzt betonen, dass wir grossen Wert auf (eine) sorgfältige Verpackung legen. Unter keinen Umständen darf der Inhalt der Sendung durch Seewasser beschädigt werden. Die Verpackung soll deshalb den beim Seetransport üblichen Normen entsprechen.
Wollen Sie bitte Ihrem Angebot den neuesten Katalog und die Preisliste beifügen.

Letter writing assignments

1 The Undersmith Co (Europe) Ltd writes to the Cleveland factory enclosing another order for flexible disk processors and parts, making several suggestions for improved packing. The last consignment contained slightly damaged ribbon cassette parts which were not packed well enough.

2. Undersmith Co Inc, Cleveland, tut es leid, dass die letzte Sendung Transportschäden aufwies. Sie bedankt sich bei Ihrer europäischen Niederlassung für die Vorschläge, die eingehend geprüft worden sind. In Zukunft werden die Teile in robustere Schachteln verpackt und zuoberst in die Kiste bzw. den Container gelegt. Jeder Behälter wird zudem mit «zerbrechlich» und mit «[diese Seite] oben» bezeichnet.

15 Transport

Road and rail carriage are the most frequently used forms of inland transport. Goods are usually handled less when conveyed by road, as they are loaded at the factory or warehouse and unloaded on arrival at their destination. Rail transport by goods train is generally cheaper, but goods often have to be reloaded from one waggon into another and may be delayed for several days, waiting for connections. Merchandise dispatched by passenger train will be delivered more quickly, but the size of the consignment is limited.

The cheapest and oldest form of transport, by inland waterways (river and canal), plays an important part in the transport of heavy cargoes. It is economical for fuel, building materials and other bulk cargoes, especially if the question of time is not so important.

Air freight, on the other hand, is used when we wish to save time. Although it is relatively expensive the great saving in time makes it worth while, and particularly so for valuable goods, samples, perishables or articles that are light in weight. Container transport provides a safe and economical method, by which large quantities of goods or frozen food can be consigned direct on special container trucks, trailer trucks or container ships.

Overseas shipments are sometimes complicated and so forwarding agents are generally employed to deal with these. Besides export and import formalities and customs clearance, flights and sailings must be selected, tonnage space booked, the goods have to be insured, collected from the consignor and loaded on board.

inland	inländisch
convey, to	übermitteln, befördern
load, to	(auf)laden
unload, to	entladen
discharge, to	entladen
connection	Verbindung
limit, to	begrenzen
fuel	Treibstoff
bulk cargo	Massengüter
save, to	sparen
perishables	leicht verderbliche Waren
employ, to	einstellen, einsetzen
customs clearance	Zollabfertigung
insure, to	versichern
consignor	Absender

Posten	item:	an article or bookkeeping entry
	lot:	a number of goods together

	to dispatch:	absenden, aufgeben (advice of dispatch)
	to send:	(ver)senden, zustellen (to send back, to send on)
	to ship:	verschiffen, versenden shipment, air shipment
liefern, schicken	to mail/ airmail:	mit der Post / Luftpost senden
	to forward:	weiterleiten, befördern (forwarding agent)
	to consign:	zusenden, liefern (consignor, consignee)
	to deliver:	liefern, abliefern

Vocabulary exercise

Choose the correct words from the list.
1 Inland transport refers mainly to ____ and ____ carriage.
2 When goods are ____ by road they are ____ less, because they are not ____ until they reach their ____.
3 By rail they may have to be ____, and time is lost between ____.
4 When ____ is dispatched by passenger train, the ____ of the consignment is usually limited.
5 Transport by water is ____ for heavy ____ like ____ and building materials.
6 Air ____ is fast, and worth while for ____ and ____ goods.
7 ____ transport is economical too, because the ____ saves on packing materials.
8 ____ agents deal with the formalities connected with ____ abroad.
9 When goods are exported, they have to be ____ and customs ____ must be arranged.

cargoes
clearance
connections
consignor
container
conveyed
destination
economical
forwarding
freight
fuel
insured
handled
merchandise
perishables
rail
reloaded
road
shipments
size
unloaded
valuable

	forwarding agent	Agent für Güterabfertigung
Spediteur	(forwarder: short form)	
	carrier	Transportunternehmer, Frachtführer

Birmingham Tool Co Ltd
224 Snow Street
Birmingham BIR OAA, England

Messrs Tiberio & Sons, S.p.A.
Via A. Dipieto 3
Turin   6 January 19..

Dear Sirs

Regarding your order No 955, we wish to inform you that our London forwarding agents, Messrs Harrington Bros, 49 Upper Thames Street, London, had the goods collected from our factory this morning. They are being shipped via London by SS MEDITERRANEAN STAR sailing from Tilbury docks on 13th of this month.

Packing: Seaworthy cases (non-returnable).
Marks & Nos: T & Co TURIN 1 - 4.

You will be receiving copies of packing lists, certificate of origin and commercial invoice from Messrs Harrington Bros. Our bank will send you the other shipping documents: set of bills of lading (3 originals), insurance certificate and sight draft.

We trust that the goods will reach you in good condition, and that this order will lead to further business.

                                        Yours faithfully

STAR STEAMSHIP LINE
BARROW, BAILEY & CO
Commercial Road
London E16 3T0

Castigliano SRL
Via Tadina 119
Firenze, Italy   27 December 19..

Dear Sirs

Thank you for your inquiry of 23 December. Our ships, AFRICAN STAR, MEDITERRANEAN STAR and EASTERN STAR call at the ports of London, Genoa and Athens fortnightly. The next sailing from Tilbury Docks is on 13 January 19.. unloading at Genoa on 21 January.

Freight rates for the shipment in question are £6 W/M (subject to alteration).

Please complete the enclosed Booking Note and return it to us by 8 January if the goods are to be on board by 12 January.

                                    Yours faithfully

                                    A Bailey

Enc

notification   *Benachrichtigung, Anzeige*
docks   *Hafen(anlagen)*
fortnightly   *vierzehntäglich*
rate   *Tarif*

Model sentences (transportation)

1. Freight rates are very high at present, as few ships are sailing on this route.
2. Please let us know the difference in rates between transport by goods train and passenger train.
3. Would you let us know the current costs for road transport.
4. The shipment has been collected today for forwarding to New York by MV Atlante.
5. As the goods are so urgently required, we have consigned them by air.
6. Since the goods are very bulky and not required immediately, they can be transported by inland waterways.
7. The goods were shipped by the MV Glenmore, cif Southampton.
8. We enclose the relevant documents: bills of lading in duplicate, consignment note, commercial invoice and import licence.
9. Please consign the goods to our address at the bonded warehouse, Frankfurt airport.
10. Delivery will be made by road to avoid frequent handling.

Sentences for translation

1. Bezugnehmend auf Ihre Anweisungen vom 10. Juli 19.. teilen wir Ihnen mit, dass die zwei Tonnen Orangen für die Verschiffung mit der SPANISH GLORY verladen worden sind. Die SPANISH GLORY fährt heute nach Glasgow ab.
2. Die Fabrik hat die bestellten Waren vor dem vereinbarten Lieferdatum abgeschickt. Nun erfahren wir, dass die Sendung immer noch in Hamburg ist und auf Verschiffung wartet [= erwartet].
3. Wollen Sie bitte die Originalkonnossemente dreifach ausfertigen und sie der First National Bank in Albington per Luftpost schicken, damit uns die Waren gegen Wechselakzept unverzüglich ausgeliefert werden.
4. Die Werkzeuge werden in der ersten Novemberwoche unfranko nach Liverpool gesandt.
5. Könnten Sie uns bitte die Frachttarife für 4 Kisten Werkzeuge à 0,3 m³ und 80 kg von London nach Genua nennen.
6. Wir legen Kopien des Ursprungszeugnisses, der Rechnung und der Einfuhrgenehmigung bei.
7. Um Zeit zu sparen haben wir unsere Spediteure beauftragt, diese Formalitäten zu erledigen.

Letters for translation

1. Von: Birmingham Tool Co. Ltd., 224 Snow Street, Birmingham BIR 0AA
   An: Schröter & Müller AG, Industriestrasse 8, 9010 St. Gallen

   17. Januar 19..

   Nachdem wir uns über Verpackungs- und Transportart eingehend erkundigt haben, können wir Ihnen folgendes mitteilen:
   Die Werkzeugmaschinen werden in wasserdichte Kisten verpackt, die sie sicherlich vor Seewasser schützen. Wir empfehlen Ihnen, die Sendung von Rotterdam aus zu verschiffen, da die Frachtkosten niedriger sind als per Bahn.
   Transport auf dem Wasserweg ist aber nur möglich, wenn die Lieferfrist nicht zu genau eingehalten werden muss. Verschiffen dauert immer etwas länger, und die Zollabfertigung im Europoort benötigt mehr Zeit als wenn der Transport per Bahn durchgeführt wird.
   Sie können sich darauf verlassen, dass wir Ihre Aufträge mit grösster Sorgfalt ausführen werden. Wir sind überzeugt, dass Sie mit dem Verkauf unserer Produkte gute Erfahrungen machen [haben] werden.

2. Von: Martin Chardonnens, Genf
   An: Smith & Sons, 35 Baker Street, London W1 7TM

   28. Juni 19..

   Die Continental Express AG meldet uns soeben, dass die Thermofax-Kopiermaschine in Genf angekommen ist.
   Für die Zollabfertigung benötigen wir folgende Papiere:

   Rechnung im Doppel
   Ursprungserklärung

   Wir werden eine Mietgebühr bezahlen müssen, wenn die Kopiermaschine nicht innert 7 Tagen abgefertigt ist. Daher bitten wir Sie dringend, uns umgehend die gewünschten Dokumente zu senden.

   Mit freundlichen Grüssen

Letter writing assignments

The Horba Designers and Workshop, Hauptstr. 78, 2500 Biel, write to the Good Timer Company, 1408 Western Broadway, San Francisco, Ca 94101 with reference to their order for gold watch straps. After investigating various possibilities of transport they have decided on air freight. Give description of packing (each watch strap wrapped in plastic, packed per dozen in cartons, then in light alloy boxes). Prices are fob Amsterdam, therefore air freight and insurance will be charged to customer. End with an assuring sentence.

16 Insurance

The purpose of insurance is to spread the losses of a few policyholders over many. Insurance services can be divided into these classes:

1 Fire insurance (including loss of profits due to fire);
2 Accident (including burglary or theft, motor or personal accident, third party liability);
3 Marine (including aviation and other methods of transport);
4 Life assurance (providing a lump sum when an insured person dies, or a pension for retirement);
5 Reinsurance of any of the above classes.

Insurance began in Britain in the 16th century with marine risk insurance. In London seamen, merchants and bankers used to meet at the coffee house of Edward Lloyd. There the association of Lloyd's underwriters was formed. Private individuals cannot deal direct with Lloyd's but must obtain insurance through a broker.

The risks covered are set out in a policy, which becomes valid as soon as it is signed by both parties and the premium paid. If, for instance, an accident occurs, the insured person reports the damage or loss and files a claim for compensation with the insurance company. The insurer will investigate the claim, and an insurance surveyor will inspect the damage, if necessary. Compensation can then be paid in full or in part, depending on the extent and cause of the damage.

spread, to	*ausbreiten, verteilen*
loss	*Verlust, Schaden*
policyholder	*Versicherungsnehmer*
due to	*wegen, verursacht durch*
burglary	*Einbruch*
theft	*Diebstahl*
motor accident	*Verkehrsunfall*
liability	*Haftung*
third party liability	*Haftpflicht*
marine insurance	*Transportversicherung*
war risk	*Kriegsrisiko*
aviation	*Luftfahrt*
lump sum	*Pauschalabfindung*
retire, to	*in Pension gehen*
reinsurance	*Rückversicherung*
merchant	*Kaufmann, Handelsherr*
banker	*Bankier*
underwriter	*Versicherer*
obtain, to	*erhalten*
set out, to	*darlegen, festsetzen*
broker	*Makler*

valid	*gültig*
premium	*Prämie*
for instance	*zum Beispiel*
file a claim, to	*Forderung einreichen, Schaden melden*
compensation	*Entschädigung*
insurer	*Versicherer*
investigate, to	*untersuchen*
surveyor	*Inspektor*
survey	*Gutachten, Umfrage*
extent	*Umfang*

Vocabulary exercise

Choose the correct words from the list.
1. The ____ of insurance is to spread risk.
2. A ____ for fire insurance also covers loss of ____ resulting from the event.
3. ____ and third party ____ fall under accident insurance.
4. Damage to goods conveyed by air is ____ under ____ insurance.
5. A life assurance can ____ a pension for ____ .
6. Insurance companies cover their ____ by means of ____ .
7. Already in the 16th century seamen, ____ and ____ arranged marine risk insurance.
8. A private individual can only ____ an insurance from Lloyds through the services of a ____ .
9. A policy describes the ____ covered and the amount of ____ payable.
10. When a claim for compensation is ____ , the insurance company sends a ____ to inspect the ____ .

bankers
broker
burglary
compensation
damage
filed
insured
liability
losses
marine
merchants
obtain
policy
profits
provide
purpose
reinsurance
retirement
risks
surveyor

Steward & Kerns Forwarding Agents
22 Upper Thames Street
London EC4 4HX

Central Insurance Co
(Marine Insurance Dept)
14a Gracechurch Street
London EC3 1LH   21 December 19..

Dear Sirs

Insurance rates

Would you please quote us your rates for insuring a consignment of 10 tons oranges, value £3,000 in transit between Valencia and London against all risks. The fruit is crated and will probably be shipped on the PATRIOT sailing 5 January.

As our clients, the Fresh Fruit Wholesalers Ltd are likely to import fruit regularly from a Valencia supplier, we should be glad to hear whether you could issue an open policy for approximately £150,000 worth annually.

                              Yours faithfully

Central Insurance Co 14a Gracechurch Street
Marine Insurance Departement London EC3 1LH

Messrs Stewart & Kerns
22 Upper Thames Street
London EC4 4HX   22 December 19..

Dear Sirs

<u>Premiums for large consignments</u>

In reply to your letter of 21st of this month, we inform you that our premium rates for the consignment of oranges mentioned would be 45 per cent to your clients' warehouse or market in London.

Would you let us know by telephone whether you wish us to cover this consignment, as time is rather short; we shall then prepare the policy accordingly.

Goods shipped by any of the approved Lines detailed on the attached list, and packed according to the usual standards, can be insured at the rate of 38 p per cent on an open policy value £150,000 per annum. This covers all risks but excludes war risk.

May we hear from you soon?

                                        Yours faithfully

                                        CENTRAL INSURANCE CO
                                        Marine Insurance Dept

Enc

The Secure Life Assurance Co Ltd
16–20 Stratford Road   Warwick CV34 4AP

Robert Ankers Esq
101 The Close
Maidenhead, Berks DJ3 9XB   4 December 19..

Dear Sir

May we ask you for a few moments of your attention?

Have you considered for how much you are insured and what your insurance covers? Does it give you enough cover to meet present needs, and does it correspond to the continually rising cost of living?

Perhaps you think that you are already paying too much in premiums for your insurance, but could this possibly be due to some overlapping? Of course, it would be worse to have gaps in your insurance cover which would bring financial disadvantages when an insured event occurs.

It would certainly be best for you to have an analysis made by a member of our staff, showing clearly whether you are effectively insured.

In order to give you full information without any obligation to you and to answer your queries, our consultant, Mr Stanley Harrington, will contact you within the next few days.

                                        Yours faithfully

                                        Counselling Group

rate	Tarif
crated	in Harrasse verpackt
issue, to	ausgeben, ausstellen (Dokument)
approximately	ungefähr
accordingly	entsprechend
approve, to	zustimmen
exclude, to	ausschliessen
replacement	Ersatz
negligence	Nachlässigkeit
adequate	angemessen, genügend
gap	Lücke
query	Rückfrage

Model sentences (insurance)

1 Our claim for compensation, enclosed, shows that damage was caused by water as well as by fire.
2 Also enclosed is a report signed by the carriers, confirming that damage to the boxes was ascertained when they were unloaded.
3 You have had your factory, warehouse and stock insured by our company for 12 years now. We would suggest a re-appraisal, so that your policy may be adjusted to present values.
4 The enclosed proposal has been prepared as a basis for discussion. We shall, of course, be pleased to suggest alternatives.
5 The PLUS plan is a new type of insurance, which allows you to adapt your benefits automatically to the rising cost of living.
6 We have pleasure in enclosing your insurance policy, duly signed. Would you be so kind as to check the details, and let us know if anything needs rectifying. If not, please countersign both copies, and return one of these to us.

Sentences for translation

1. Diese zerbrechliche Sendung muss zu einem höheren Tarif versichert werden.
2. Wir werden mit dieser Police nicht in der Lage sein, Kriegsrisiko/Einbruch zu decken.
3. Die Untersuchung hat ergeben, dass ein Teil der Sendung fehlt, nämlich die Kisten Nr. 13 und 14.
4. Eine Versicherungspolice wird rechtsgültig, wenn beide Parteien unterschrieben haben und die Prämie bezahlt ist.
5. Wir vermuten, dass Ihre Beschwerde auf einen Irrtum zurückzuführen ist; würden Sie sich deshalb bitte mit der Versicherungsgesellschaft in Verbindung setzen.

6. Unter diesen Umständen bitten wir Sie, die Ladung genau zu untersuchen und uns den Prüfungsbefund so bald wie möglich zukommen zu lassen.
7. Ohne diesen Bericht können wir keinen Anspruch auf Schadenersatz akzeptieren.
8. Vielleicht gibt es Lücken in Ihrer Versicherungsdeckung, oder dann zahlen Sie zu viel an Prämien. Unser Versicherungsfachmann wird Sie gerne beraten.
9. Wir haben Ihnen einen Vorschlag zur weiteren Diskussion vorbereitet; natürlich sind mehrere Alternativen möglich.
10. Ihre Versicherungspolice Nr. CP 102/372.1 ist nun seit 10 Jahren in Kraft. Mit Blick auf (die) Inflation raten wir Ihnen, mit unserem Berater eine Neueinschätzung zu besprechen.

Letters for translation

1. Von: Britannia Insurance Ltd, 85 Lombard Street, London EC3P 4NR.
   An: Messrs Robertson & Co, 7 Upper Thames Street, London EC5A 5HX.

   20. August 19..

   Sehr geehrte Herren

   Wie vereinbart, haben wir Ihren Gebäudeversicherungsvertrag (für Fabrik und Lagerhaus) den heutigen Werten angepasst, und wir legen die Police, ordnungsgemäss unterschrieben, im Doppel bei.
   Wären Sie so gut, die einzelnen Bestimmungen [= Einzelheiten] zu prüfen und uns mitzuteilen, falls irgend etwas berichtigt werden muss. Falls nicht, wollen Sie bitte Original und Kopie gegenzeichnen und die Kopie an uns zurücksenden.

   Mit freundlichen Grüssen

2. Von: Richard Stadel, Wollzeile 34, 9450 Altstätten, Schweiz
   An: Northern Insurance Company, Transport Insurance Dpt, 104 Fleet Street, London EC4P 2NR

   12. März 19..

   Sehr geehrte Herren

   Am 22. Februar kaufte ich in Londen eine antike silberne Kaffeekanne zum Preis von 182 Pfund.
   Der Versand wurde durch den Antiquitätenhändler in London besorgt. Bevor ich Londen verliess, habe ich die Sendung bei Ihrer Gesellschaft

versichern lassen. Die Versicherungspolice deckt sowohl Verlust als auch Beschädigung des Gegenstandes bis zum Betrag von £182.
Beim Eintreffen der Sendung in Altstätten bemerkte ich, dass der Deckel der Kaffeekanne fehlte. Eine schriftliche Anfrage beim Händler in London und eine Untersuchung bei den Zollbehörden waren erfolglos.
Da ich eine Schadenersatzforderung einreichen möchte, bitte ich Sie, mir die notwendigen Formulare zuzustellen.

Mit freundlichen Grüssen

Letter writing assignments

Undersmith Co (Europe) AG informiert The General Marine Insurance Co, 314 281st Street, Brooklyn, New York, NY 11217, darüber, dass Undersmith Cleveland die Verpackung der zu verschiffenden Waren verbessert hat. Nun wird angefragt, ob sich dadurch nicht eine reduzierte Versicherungsprämie ergebe.

17 Complaints

In spite of good organization, responsible work, control systems and supervision on the part of the staff, certain things can go wrong with the execution of orders or in connection with other matters.

A good business manager realizes that this may occur within his own company, and will show understanding when mistakes occur in his supplier's firm. If he feels he has the right to complain, the purpose of his letter is to have matters put right. An angry letter, through which he may 'let off steam' or show his feelings, will usually not achieve this. The best way is to state the facts – to give details of the order, to confirm the delivery dates arranged, to specify the type of goods required, to report any damage incurred, or to list the documents required – and to stipulate that matters be put right.

If the first complaint is made by phone or telex, he should also put the facts in writing: there may be repetitions, and then he will appreciate being able to refer to correspondence.

complaint	*Beschwerde, Mängelrüge*
responsible	*verantwortlich, zuverlässig*
supervision	*Aufsicht, Kontrolle*
have, to	*hier: veranlassen*
achieve, to	*erreichen*
arrange, to	*absprechen*
incur, to	*erleiden, auf sich laden*
stipulate, to	*ausbedingen*

Vocabulary exercise

Choose the correct words from the list.
1 Even in an efficient ____ there may be insufficient ____ by some employees.
2 Mistakes can sometimes ____ during the ____ of an order.
3 An experienced businessman knows that things may go wrong and will not write an ____ complaint.
4 He may, however, expect the ____ to ____ the goods in good condition.
5 The purpose of a ____ is to ____ matters put right.
6 It is important to ____ the facts exactly: to report the damage ____, or to ____ to delivery dates ____.
7 When the wrong goods are supplied, the customer should ____ what he ____.
8 He can ____ that mistakes are corrected.

arranged
deliver
complaint
company
execution
have
incurred
occur
refer
requires
specify
state
stipulate
supervision
supplier
unreasonable

133

Mercuria School of Business Studies
Hejrevej 25
DK 2400 Copenhagen NV

```
The Undersmith Co (Europe) AG        EXPRESS
12 Gotthardstrasse
6300 Zug
Switzerland                          6 September 19..
```

Dear Sirs

We are surprised that we have not yet received the sixty typewriters ordered from you on 2 July of this year.

As you will remember, the order was placed on condition that we should receive the machines by 4 September, in time for the commencement of the term. School starts on 8 September, and I urge you to send them without delay, so that they will be here by the end of this week at the latest. If they are not in our possession by then, please regard the order as cancelled.

                                            Yours faithfully

THE UNDERSMITH CO (EUROPE) AG
12 Gotthardstrasse
6300 Zug, Switzerland

Messrs Verbrugge & Son
De Ruyterkade 193
1011 AC Amsterdam
The Netherlands   September 7, 19..

Gentlemen:

I refer to this morning's telephone conversation, when I reported the non-delivery of the sixty typewriters which we dispatched to the Mercuria School of Business Studies on the 2nd of this month. During the conversation Mr Verbrugge admitted that there had been an oversight on your part. We trust, in accordance with your promise, that the goods have now been delivered to our customer.

As you will remember, this is not the first complaint we have made; there have been some other instances of delay in delivery of late. For this reason we must point out that we shall have to take our business elsewhere if your carrier service does not improve.

                                        Sincerely yours

Clarkson Ltd
76 Rover Street
Lancaster LB2 7YZ

Messrs Jackson Bros
91 Newton Road
Buxton, Derby L528 9BW   13 April 19..

Dear Sirs

We have received the consignment of artificial silk covered by your Invoice No. 1320. On unpacking it we have ascertained that the quality is below the standard of that of the samples which your representative, Mr Robinson, showed us. To prove our statement, we are enclosing one of these samples and a cutting of the material received yesterday. You will notice, as we did, that the material is inferior; it is lighter in weight, and the colours are not so bright.

Although this quality is not really suitable for our customers, we shall try to dispose of these goods elsewhere. We are, however, not prepared to pay the full price you charge, as this material is not at all what we ordered. We suggest your reducing the invoice amount by 25%. Otherwise we shall have to return the consignment to you immediately, carriage forward.

We await your decision by return.

                                        Yours faithfully

Enc: Sample and cutting

FREE UNIVERSITY VIENNA
Departement of Physics
Helmutstrasse 27
A – 1232 Vienna 23

Instrument Division
Electronics Associates Inc
Culver City, Calif 90230
USA   November 15, 19..

Dear Dr Franklin:

Nearly a year ago we had a P-60 computer supplied to our laboratory. In working with it since its arrival we have had to use the services of your engineer four times.

Other physics laboratories do not appear to have had so much trouble with their equipment. I admit your service engineer has always found the cause of the complaint and has managed to put the equipment into working order. However, in the course of this last year we have lost two months of working time, waiting for repairs to be carried out, which has been most inconvenient.

Our one year's guarantee will be expiring next month, and I should prefer not to keep this equipment. It appears that we have simply been unfortunate in receiving one of a series that is not up to standard. Therefore we would like to send it back to your factory and have it replaced by a new computer. I should be willing to pay a rental of some kind in proportion to the actual period of use.

In the past I have often recommended your products to scientists in other laboratories. I hope you will find a solution which will enable me to do so again in the future.

                                         Very truly yours

                                         Professor G Keller

admit, to	zugeben
instance	Beispiel, Fall
improve, to	verbessern
commencement	Beginn
cancel, to	annullieren
inferior	minderwertig
carriage forward	unfranko
physics	naturwissenschaftlich
equipment	Apparatur, Ausrüstung
inconvenient	lästig, ungelegen
rental	Mietbetrag
solution	Lösung

---

erwarten	to expect:	als wahrscheinlich erachten
	to await:	auf etwas warten, abwarten

1. I expect there will be a shortage soon.
2. We are awaiting your early reply.

Model sentences

1 Some of the goods you supplied were of inferior quality. We are returning them by airmail, and would ask you to replace them by return.
2 On unpacking the cases we found that they contained 800 tins of strawberry jam instead of the 80 we ordered on 14 March (your order confirmation No 17310 dated 30 March).
3 Your last consignment was unsatisfactory in two respects.
4 Some of the goods appear to have been damaged in transit.
5 We have not yet received delivery of the machines which should have been in our possession on 1 October.
6 This delay is involving us in a loss of business. Unless we receive the material by 2 January, we must refuse acceptance.
7 The amount shown in the invoice, £108, should read £10.80. Would you please send us a rectified invoice.
8 The quality does not correspond to the patterns on the basis of which we placed our order; we are prepared to keep these only if you reduce the price by 20%.
9 Please look into the non-delivery of the equipment which we ordered on 10 August.
10 We hope that a repetition of the trouble will be avoided in future.

Sentences for translation

1. Wir bedauern, Ihnen mitteilen zu müssen, dass Ihre kürzliche Lieferung unter dem üblichen Standard war.

2. Da Sie die vor fünf Monaten bestellten Waren noch nicht geliefert haben, sind wir widerstrebend gezwungen, die Bestellung zu annullieren.
3. Ihre Sendung wurde heute geliefert und war in Ordnung, mit (der) Ausnahme zweier fehlender Ersatzteile S 113.
4. Wir verlassen uns darauf, dass Sie so bald als möglich Ersatzteile schicken werden.
5. Falls die Angelegenheit nicht zur Zufriedenheit geregelt wird, werden wir Ihnen keine weiteren Bestellungen mehr aufgeben.
6. Seit wir die Anlage im September erhalten haben, war Ihr Servicetechniker zweimal hier, um Reparaturen auszuführen.
7. Wir scheinen eine Maschine erhalten zu haben, die von minderer Qualität ist.
8. Zum Beweis unserer Aussage senden wir Ihnen ein Bild des defekten Teils.
9. Sie werden uns zustimmen, dass dieses Material in keiner Art und Weise das ist, was wir bestellten.
10. Darum erwarten wir, dass Sie uns einen speziellen Preisnachlass von 20% einräumen [= erlauben].
11. Falls wir die Möbel bis zum Ende des Monats nicht erhalten, werden wir die Annahme verweigern.
12. Der Schaden scheint durch unzulängliche Verpackung verursacht worden zu sein.

Letters for translation

Von: John Simon, Church Road, Burgess Hill, Sussex BF9 4RR
An: Martin & Söhne, Möbelfabrik, Hollow Oak Road, London SW99 4RP
12. Oktober 19..

Wir bestätigen unser heutiges Telegramm wie folgt:

Verweigere Möbel (der) Rechnung 310328. Minderwertige Qualität. Baldige Besichtigung erwünscht.
Leider müssen wir Ihnen mitteilen, dass wir sehr enttäuscht sind über die Beschaffenheit der uns am 10. Oktober gelieferten Möbel. Diese weicht deutlich [= greatly] von der Qualität früherer Lieferungen ab, und wir können unseren guten Ruf durch Auslieferung dieser Möbel an unsere Kundschaft nicht aufs Spiel setzen.
Diese Situation verursacht uns grosse Unannehmlichkeiten, da wir einigen guten Kunden Lieferung zu Beginn des nächsten Monats versprochen haben. Darum würden wir Ihren Vertreter gerne so bald als möglich sehen, um die Angelegenheit zu besprechen. Dann kann er auch die beanstandeten [= abgelehnten] Möbel inspizieren, die sich im Lagerhaus unseres Spediteurs befinden.
Wir verlassen uns darauf, dass Sie die Beschwerde sofort behandeln werden und grüssen Sie freundlich

Letter writing assignments

1. The Undersmith Co (UK), 33 Watling Street, London EC1 2MK hat zwei defekte Drucker erhalten. Informieren Sie die europäische Niederlassung in Zug darüber und verlangen Sie die Reparatur oder den Ersatz der fehlerhaften Geräte.
2. Beschweren Sie sich in einem Brief über Transportschäden, die vermutlich wegen unsachgemässer Verpackung entstanden sind. Beschreiben Sie den Zustand der Ware, und machen Sie einen Vorschlag zur Schadensregulierung.

18 Dealing with complaints

When a complaint is received, the matter should be investigated promptly. In the case of a delay in delivery the customer has a right to know when he can expect the goods ordered. Where goods have been damaged he must be informed whether and how he will be compensated; this is often the insurance company's obligation. If mistakes have been made in paperwork, it is relatively simple to send a rectified document. If the standard of goods supplied is inferior, some agreement must be made on a reduction in price, or replacements have to be supplied. Where the seller is at fault he should admit this, apologize and settle the matter to the buyer's satisfaction.

There are, however, cases when a complaint is not justified. The writer of a letter replying to a complaint of this kind has to write most carefully and tactfully when rejecting the customer's claim. Under some circumstances it is possible to make a compromise. His long-term point of view is to maintain a good business relationship. Many companies actually encourage customers to inform them whenever they are not completely satisfied with the goods or services received. They welcome criticism as an opportunity to improve goodwill.

agreement	Übereinkunft
be at fault, to	schuld sein
apologize, to	entschuldigen
justify, to	rechtfertigen
reject, to	ablehnen, zurückweisen
maintain, to	(aufrecht)erhalten
encourage, to	ermutigen

Vocabulary exercise

Choose the correct words from the list.

1 A seller receiving a ____ should ____ the cause as soon as he can.
2 If delivery has been ____, the customer will want to know when goods will be ____.
3 It is the ____ company's duty to compensate for damaged goods, though here too the ____ should offer whatever assistance he can.
4 A ____ document can easily be supplied if a mistake has been made in ____.
5 The situation is more complex if ____ goods have been supplied; perhaps ____ can be sent, or the seller may ____ to a ____ in price.
6 When a complaint is not ____, it may be difficult to ____ the matter satisfactorily.
7 This type of claim often has to be ____ by the seller.
8 At the same time, however, it is important to ____ a good business ____.

agree
complaint
delayed
dispatched
inferior
insurance
investigate
justified
maintain
paperwork
rectified
reduction
rejected
relationship
replacements
settle
supplier

Verbrugge & Son, Carriers & Forwarding Agents
De Ruyterkade 193   1011 AC Amsterdam

Mr Beat Weitner
The Undersmith Co (Europe) AG
12 Gotthardstrasse
6300 Zug
Switzerland   8 September 19..

Dear Mr Weitner

As I explained to you during our telephone conversation on 6 September, our failure to deliver the typewriters to your customer in Haarlem was, I regret, due to an oversight.

Our driver had collected the consignment on Friday afternoon but, on delivering it to the school on the same day, found it closed. The goods were taken back to our warehouse where, on Monday last, they were unfortunately left behind.

The month of September is perhaps the busiest of the year in our trade; in addition, we are short-staffed at present. Of course, we accept full responsibility for the mistake, for which we apologize. We are taking steps to ensure that such errors will be avoided in future.

                                        Yours truly

                                        T Verbrugge

Electronics Associates Inc.   Culver City
California 90230

Professor G. Keller
Department of Physics
Free University
A-1011 Vienna, Austria

December 10, 19..

Dear Professor Keller:

It is rather upsetting when an old and valued customer like yourself feels that he is not receiving the quality of equipment and service which we always try to give.

After referring the question to our European service department, I would like to pass on our engineer's views. The purpose of his first visit last January was to install the computer and instruct your staff as to its use. Afterwards he was requested to come again as, due to incorrect operation, a part had become defective. At your last request, two weeks ago, our engineer went to Austria again to make some minor adjustments.

Our system of quality control ensures that all our computers are up to standard. It appears to us that lack of ability or training of your assistants could have something to do with the difficulties you have been experiencing, or perhaps our instructions for use were not quite clear to you. If you wish, we will arrange for a member of your staff to use equipment of the same type at our German agency or at some scientific institute elsewhere.

We wish to be fair, but, unfortunately, must reject your claim for a new one. Our offer to have a member of your staff work on our equipment may serve as proof of our continued assistance, now and in the future.

Very truly yours

G. Franklin
Instrument Division

sincere	*aufrichtig*
in addition	*darüber hinaus, zusätzlich*
ensure, to	*sicherstellen*
upset, to	*bestürzen, aus der Fassung bringen*
view	*Ansicht, Meinung*
operation	*Bedienung*
minor	*geringfügig*
adjustment	*Einstellung, Regulierung*
lack	*Fehlen, Mangel*
agency	*Agentur, Vertretung*
proof	*Beweis*

Model sentences (answers to complaints)

1 We very much regret the loss of business which the delay has caused.
2 While we greatly regret the inconvenience, we feel sure you will understand it was due to circumstances beyond our control.
3 Though we are in no way responsible for this unfortunate situation, we will naturally do everything in our power to remedy it.
4 Please accept our sincere apologies for the mistake in your order.
5 We apologize for the delay and very much appreciate your helpful attitude.
6 We are sorry to hear that our latest consignment has not found a ready market.
7 We have investigated your complaint and have ascertained that an error was made in our dispatch control department.
8 Your claim has been passed on to our insurance company, who will get in touch with you directly.
9 If you keep the damaged goods, we are prepared to invoice them at 50% below the original price.
10 Action has been taken at once to ensure that no more mistakes of this kind will occur in future.

Sentences for translation

1. Wenn (die) Lieferung sich aus irgendeinem Grund verzögert, muss der Kunde darüber informiert werden, wann er die bestellte Ware erwarten kann.
2. Eine Ersatzforderung für beschädigte Waren wird oft unter den Bedingungen der Transportversicherung durch das Versicherungsunternehmen beglichen.
3. Die Radios, die Sie erhielten, hätten an einen anderen Kunden geliefert werden sollen.
4. Würden Sie bitte die Sendung unfranko an uns zurückschicken.

5. Sie können [= dürfen] diese Kleider zu einem reduzierten Preis behalten; unsere angepasste Rechnung liegt bei.
6. Obwohl die Garantiezeit abgelaufen ist, möchten wir Ihnen helfen, indem wir diese Reparaturen kostenlos durchführen.
7. Unsere Überprüfung hat keinerlei Mängel aufgezeigt, so dass für Sie kein Grund vorliegt, die Radios an uns zurückzuschicken.
8. Sie werden verstehen, dass wir unter diesen Umständen keine Verantwortung für den Verlust übernehmen können.
9. Bei der erneuten Überprüfung des Materials haben wir festgestellt, dass Ihre Beschwerde berechtigt ist. Wir senden Ihnen sofort Ersatz.
10. Bitte nehmen Sie unsere Entschuldigung für diesen Fehler entgegen. Wir unternehmen Schritte, um sicherzustellen, dass so was [= es] nicht wieder vorkommt.

Letters for translation

Von: Martin & Sohn, Möbelfabrik, Hollow Oak Road, London SW18 7HL
An: John Simon, Church Road, Burgess Hill, Sussex BF9 4RR
16. Oktober 19..

Sehr geehrter Herr Simon

Dieses Schreiben betrifft die Überprüfung, die ich gestern im Lagerhaus Ihres Spediteurs vorgenommen habe.
Es scheint tatsächlich so, dass Sie zwei Schreibtische, einen Tisch und eine Garnitur Büchergestelle erhalten haben, die nicht befriedigend verfertigt wurden. Wir sind der Sache nachgegangen und haben herausgefunden, dass diese Möbel wegen der Krankheit eines Kontrolleurs nicht ordnungsgemäss überprüft worden sind. Wir haben (die) Ersatzmöbel heute versandt, und ich habe mich vergewissert, dass diese Möbelstücke in makellosem Zustand sind. Der Transportunternehmer wird die mangelhaften Möbel bei der Auslieferung mitnehmen. Entschuldigen Sie bitte dieses Versehen. Wir hoffen, dass Sie vollkommen zufrieden sein werden, wenn Sie in Zukunft bei uns Büromöbel bestellen.

Mit freundlichen Grüssen

Letter writing assignments

1. Howard & Sons, 242 Manchester Road, Liverpool LB4 7D2, schreiben an J. Petersen GmbH, Ringweg 220, D-4600 Dortmund.
   Die von der Firma bestellten Baumwollballen – bezeichnet mit 1/30 P.C. – sind am 30. Mai auf der SS Friesland in Liverpool eingetroffen. Howard &

Sons akzeptierten die Ladung, obwohl drei Ballen stark beschädigt waren, und zwar dermassen, dass fast die Hälfte von deren Inhalt verlustig gegangen ist. Die Firma verlangt deshalb eine Reduktion des Rechnungsbetrages um 35%.

2. J. Petersen GmbH antwortet Howard & Sons am 3. Juni, wobei sie sich für die Annahme der Sendung bedanken. Eine Gutschrift für die verlustig gegangene Ware ist beigefügt. Zukünftige Bestellungen werden noch sorgfältiger abgewickelt; trotzdem sind solche Vorfälle natürlich nie ganz auszuschliessen.

19 Marketing and distribution

If trade and business are to be successful, goods have to be made available to a consumer who wants them in his vicinity at the price he is prepared to pay. Marketing serves to discover what consumers want. It entails the study of their needs, knowledge of competitors' products, advertising and selling strategies, and arranging for distribution.

Some forms of wholesaling have declined in the last few decades in favour of more direct selling through subsidiaries and branches. But importers and agencies have their place too when the producer wants to open and maintain a market abroad. They are expected to know, or to find out what customers in their area want – often by means of market research and test marketing – and to handle sales and delivery in their territory.

Producers seeking a distributor or agent abroad frequently advertise in trade journals, or find one through the medium of a chamber of commerce or commercial department of their consulate. When they come to terms, they draw up an agreement. The importer may work as a sole distributor doing business on a consignment basis, or as an agent on his own account for several manufacturers. He may also be appointed as a representative, working for a salary and/or earning commission. In all these cases he may receive some financial backing and advertising material from his supplier.

vicinity	Nähe, Nachbarschaft
entail, to	beinhalten
wholesaling	Grosshandel
decline, to	abnehmen
decade	Jahrzehnt
subsidiary	Tochterunternehmen
branch	Filiale
territory	Gebiet
medium	Vermittlung, vermittels
chamber of commerce	Handelskammer
come to terms, to	sich einig werden
sole	alleinig
on his/her own account	auf eigene Rechnung
backing	Rückhalt, Unterstützung

Vocabulary exercise

Choose the correct words from the list.
1 Marketing is a systematic way of discovering ____ needs, taking account of ____ products.
2 It also entails plans for ____ strategies, and ____ distribution.

abroad
account
agencies
agreement
arranging

3 In the last few decades direct selling through ____ and ____ has increased.
4 Local ____ or importers can also play a part in opening up new markets ____.
5 They often find out through market ____ what their ____ want, what products are in ____.
6 A ____ or a ____ can be helpful in finding a suitable distributor.
7 When the ____ and the distributor come to terms, they draw up an ____.
8 A ____ distributor frequently works on a ____ basis on his own ____.
9 A representative is more closely connected with his ____, earning a salary or ____.

branches
chamber of commerce
commission
competitors'
consignment
consulate
consumers'
customers
demand
manufacturer
research
selling
sole
subsidiaries
supplier

The Undersmith European business started when after World War Two Mr Sigrist offered his services as an agent. Here is the letter in which he did so.

Werner Sigrist
Zurlindenstr. 53
Zürich/Switzerland

                          Undersmith Typewriter Co Inc
                          52 Third Avenue
                          Cleveland, Ohio
                          USA

                          14 September 1946

Gentlemen:

There is a brisk demand in Europe for office machinery, especially typewriters and adding machines.

I wish to offer you my services as a commission agent for Switzerland. Having dealt in office supplies and stationery for several years, I have excellent connections in the trade and am familiar with the varying requirements and conditions all over the country. Showrooms in Zurich, Berne and Geneva, and a staff of capable salesmen are available to demonstrate and sell your products in this territory. My organization is fairly small as yet, but is developing. Naturally, we are experienced in marketing procedures, import regulations, customs formalities and shipping, and I have some new ideas for attracting more customers.

An alternative would be to appoint me as your sole distributor, doing business on a consignment basis.
I hope that I can be of help to you in increasing your turnover by promoting sales in Europe.

                          Very truly yours

                          W. Sigrist

Walkwell Footwear plc   Northampton N19 3AF
35 Wellington Square   England

Anglo-Canadian Chamber of Commerce
Rue Hotel-de-Ville
Quebec, Canada   September 15, 19..

Gentlemen:

In order to widen our markets abroad we should like to get into touch with a firm or individual willing to represent us in Canada.

Would you let us have names and addresses of reputable dealers, well connected in the shoe and leather business, with good facilities for distribution in Canada. We can offer them a high quality product with excellent selling prospects.

We thank you for your endeavors on our behalf.

                                                  Very truly yours

Walkwell Footwear plc　　　Northampton N19 3AF
35 Wellington Square　　　　　England

Messrs Smart & Bossman
Nr Clock Gate
Vancouver, Canada　　　　　　October 18, 19..

Gentlemen:

From the description of your business activities, we feel that your firm would be the right one to represent us in Canada. We, in turn, can offer you regular supplies of shoes and boots of a superior quality - products that will please your customers, and please you.

We suggest the terms of an agreement to be as follows:
- You are to act as our representatives, selling our products in the whole of Canada and Alaska.
- You would receive a commission of 10% on the net proceeds of goods sold.
- Accounts Sales are to be submitted monthly.
- Goods to be supplied against acceptance of Bill of Exchange drawn on you quarterly.
- An amount of £1800 a month will be paid by our company towards your travelling expenses, public relations and overheads. According to English business practice overhead expenses comprise office rent, staff salaries, postages and telephone.

If these terms are acceptable we shall draw up an agreement accordingly.

Our marketing manager, Mr G Rutherford, will be visiting the US and Canada next spring, and would like to discuss with you the questions of sales promotion and advertising. In the meantime, we look forward to entering into business with you and cooperation to our mutual profit.

　　　　　　　　　　　　　　　　　Yours truly

brisk	*lebhaft*
add, to	*beifügen*
reputable	*angesehen*
prospects	*Aussichten*
endeavo(u)r	*Bemühung*
on our behalf	*für uns, zu unseren Gunsten*
act, to	*auftreten*
proceeds	*Erlös*
quarterly	*vierteljährlich*
comprise, to	*umfassen*
rent	*Miete*
mutual	*gegenseitig*

Model sentences (marketing and distribution)

1. Would you let us have your opinion on the state of the market in your country.
2. As you know local conditions, we would welcome some precise information on current prices of the following goods.
3. Do you think our products would sell well in your area?
4. Your advice would help us to come to a decision on potential markets and a selling strategy.
5. Our market research has shown that there are several growth regions in this area.
6. You should therefore plan to be well represented by a sole distributor with local agents.
7. As a result of over-production in this line, the market is at present saturated.
8. Your prices are really competitive here, and we judge the prospects to be good.
9. Our knowledge of the local market leads us to believe that your goods, backed by suitable advertising, would have a ready sale in this country.
10. It is gratifying to know that our product is being well received at your end.
11. The agency we are looking for should have experience in this line and have contacts with prospective customers.
12. Please inform us if you are interested in representing us, and what volume of turnover you expect to handle in the first year.

Sentences for translation

1. Wir suchen einen Vertreter, der für uns in Norditalien Marktforschung betreiben kann.
2. Als Hersteller elektronischer Informationssysteme können wir Ihnen erstklassige Produkte mit ausgezeichneten Verkaufsaussichten anbieten.
3. Als bekannter Büromöbelimporteur haben wir Ausstellräume und Verkaufspersonal in den wichtigsten Städten.

4. Obwohl in diesem Sortiment starke Konkurrenz herrscht [= gibt], glaube ich, dass dieses Produkt – unterstützt durch gute Werbung – in Ihrer Region gut verkauft werden kann.
5. Bitte lassen Sie uns die Bedingungen wissen, unter denen Sie als unser alleiniger Zwischenhändler auftreten würden.
6. Ihre Aktivitäten waren für die Umsatzsteigerung von grosser Hilfe.
7. In Übereinstimmung mit dem am gestrigen Treffen vereinbarten Abkommen [Abmachungen] haben wir einen Agenturvertrag entworfen.
8. Einige Käufer im Westen des Landes haben nicht so viele Bestellungen aufgegeben wie wir erwartet hatten.
9. Die Qualität der Produkte Ihrer Konkurrenz ist nicht sehr gut, so dass die Einrichtung einer neuen Niederlassung gerechtfertigt scheint.

Letters for translation

1. Von: American Electric Co Inc, Industrial Way, Morrison, Illinois 61270
   An: W. Romain S. A., Natalplatz 7, 2503 Biel
   1. März 19..

   Sehr geehrter Herr Romain

   Danke für Ihre Anfrage vom 25. Februar.
   Sie sind mit unseren Produkten in Amerika vertraut geworden und fragen uns, ob Sie eine Vertretung für diese Produkte in der Schweiz errichten [= öffnen] könnten.

   Wir möchten (Ihnen gegenüber) betonen, dass wir für unsere Produkte in Westeuropa vertreten werden durch:

   Etablissements Lenoir et Cie
   52 Rue du Temple
   Paris, France

   und wir würden Ihnen raten, sich mit dieser Firma in Verbindung zu setzen. Soweit wir wissen, haben sie noch keinen Vertreter in der Schweiz, und Sie könnten möglicherweise mit dieser Firma zu einer Einigung kommen.

   Mit freundlichen Grüssen

   Kopie an: Ets. Lenoir et Cie.

2. Von: EMCO Inc., Vancouver, Canada
   An: Walkwell Footwear PLC, Northampton NI9 3AF, England

   21. September 19..

   Sehr geehrte Herren

   Es freut uns zu hören, dass Ihnen die Handelskammer in Quebec unsere Adresse gegeben hat.
   Sie haben einen ausgezeichneten Ruf in ganz Europa, und darum freut es uns, Ihnen unsere Zusammenarbeit beim Verkauf Ihrer Schuhe in Kanada anzubieten. Wie Sie richtigerweise annehmen, bietet unser Land mit seinem rauhen [= strengen] Klima ein ausgezeichnetes Verkaufspotential für Ihre Produkte.
   Bis jetzt hatten wir hauptsächlich Vertretungen für Handtaschen und andere Lederartikel.
   Beiliegend finden Sie eine Liste mit einigen Referenz-Adressen und mit Namen unserer Stammkunden. Etwa 70% unserer Kundschaft besteht aus Warenhäusern, Ladenketten und Schuhgeschäften, über ganz Kanada und Alaska verteilt.
   Sie können sicher sein, dass wir Ihre Interessen so gut wie möglich fördern werden, und wir sind überzeugt, dass wir im Verkauf Ihrer Produkte erfolgreich sein werden.
   Wir hoffen, bald von Ihnen zu hören.

   Mit freundlichen Grüssen

Letter writing assignments

1. Eine Marktforschung ergibt, dass Ihre Uhren in Florida vermutlich gut verkauft werden könnten. Verfassen Sie einen Inseratetext für das Fachblatt «Jewellery International», in dem Sie sich nach einem passenden Agenten umsehen, der Ihre Uhren dort vertreiben soll.

2. Einer der Interessenten ist Peter Westbury, 17 Rhodes John Boulevard, Melbourne, Florida 32091, USA.
   Informieren Sie ihn über Ihr Sortiment, und sagen Sie ihm, für welches Uhrenmodell Sie aufgrund der beigefügten Marktstudie die besten Verkaufschancen sehen. Fragen Sie ihn nach seiner Ansicht.

20 Sales promotion and advertising

It is not good business to wait for customers to come to you. Every good businessman knows that he must promote sales by improving or expanding his markets, employing salesmen, and by increasing consumer demand. A marketing consultant can be of great help here; he will do market research, will study consumer behaviour, market requirements and competition. He can also advise on distribution to wholesalers and retailers, and the presentation or packaging of goods.

In order to inform the public and to stimulate more people to buy, a company will advertise its products. A large company may have its own marketing specialist or publicity manager. Where this is not the case a good advertising agent will help his client in choosing the best advertising medium, or media, according to the budget available and the type of goods.

There are, for example, products that everybody uses: food, clothing, toothpaste. These are advertised in daily newspapers and popular magazines, and by means of commercials on television. More specialized articles that are bought by a smaller number of people are advertised in other media. A motoring journal, for example, has a smaller circulation than a popular magazine, and advertising here for garage equipment and tyres is cheaper and more likely to reach the appropriate consumer. If a group of users is still smaller, sales letters can be sent to prospective buyers by using a mailing list of past customers.

An advertising agent will propose an advertising campaign based on a suitable mix of media, with repetitions. He will check on the effectiveness of, for instance, poster and cinema advertising, the number of entries for a contest announced in leaflets, and the responses to direct mail advertising by sales letters.

promote, to	fördern
expand, to	ausbreiten
behaviour	Verhalten, Betragen
commercial	Werbesendung, Werbespot
circulation	Auflage
equipment	Ausrüstung
tyre	Pneu
appropriate	geeignet, passend
mailing list	Versandliste, Adressliste
campaign	Kampagne, (Werbe)feldzug
media mix	Kombination des Medieneinsatzes
entry	Einsendung, Eingang
contest	Wettbewerb

Vocabulary exercise

Choose the correct words from the list.
1 A businessman can promote sales by ____ his market.
2 Sales ____ is important in order to increase ____ demand.
3 Marketing includes the study of consumer ____, market ____ and ____.
4 The choice of advertising ____ depends on the budget ____ and the type of goods.
5 It may be a popular ____ for something like ____ or a small journal for ____ articles.
6 A mailing ____ of past customers can be used for direct ____ advertising.
7 An advertising ____ is usually based on a ____ mix of various media.
8 ____ to advertising are analysed to check its ____.
9 Manufacturers make more and more use of ____ on TV.

available
behaviour
campaign
commercials
competiton
consumer
effectiveness
expanding
list
magazine
mail
media
promotion
requirements
responses
specialized
suitable
toothpaste

Hal Hutcheson Advertising Agency
14 Main Street
Montreal

Mr C Smart
c/o EMCO Inc.
Nr Clock Gate
Vancouver   January 25, 19..

Dear Mr Smart:

It was a great pleasure meeting you last week, and I welcomed the opportunity we had to discuss the various aspects of sales promotion and the publicity of your All-weather shoes in Canada.

As promised, I am sending you enclosed a draft which describes details of the fall/winter advertising plan. Your wishes concerning press advertisements (newspaper and magazine insertions) have been followed exactly. The extent of movie advertising has been reduced to allow for wider poster display in shopping districts throughout the country.

On comparing our estimate with your original budget, you will see that the amount of $6,300 is left for direct mail advertising and point of sale material.

By the middle of February we shall let you have a more detailed account of the latter items. But we should go ahead with booking ad space quite soon, and would therefore appreciate having your approval of the general advertising plan and estimate.

We shall be in touch with you again.

                                       Very truly yours

                                       Hal Hutcheson
                                       Executive Manager

Enc

Smart & Bossmann
Near Clock Gate
Vancouver

May 7, 19..

Gentlemen:

Interest

This fall and winter more and more customers will come into your store asking for ALL-WEATHER shoes. And you will want to show them these shoes for the whole family - footwear that will sell itself, and bring you handsome profits.

Sales message

ALL-WEATHER are the hard-wearing town and country shoes that are just right for a cold climate and rough country like ours. These, as well as climbing boots and other sports shoes, are made in England, the country that specializes in fine workmanship and superior leather.

Conviction

Your customers will know all about our shoes and boots. We shall have told them through a program of national advertising, which is beginning this September. Don't you want to have these shoes in your store window? Of course you do! For, if consumers don't find the things they want in your store, they'll go to your competitor. We shall be able to help you with window display material, too.

Action

We have enough stocks on hand to supply your needs, especially if you place your order soon.
Fill out the enclosed card, and our representative will show you our selection. Or, if you should like to save time, just complete the enclosed order blank, and within four weeks' time you will be among the first successful ALL-WEATHER retailers.

Very truly yours

draft	*Entwurf*
estimate	*Schätzung, Voranschlag*
ad	*Inserat*
display	*Auslage*
handsome	*hübsch, stattlich*

Note: The words *store* (= shop), *fall* (= autumn), *program, fill out, order blank* (= form) are words used in Canada and USA.
See also pages 19–21.

Model sentences (promotion and advertising)

1 The marketing consultants' findings showed that our improvements would justify the higher prices calculated.
2 According to the terms of reference, the market survey is to include questionnaires to consumers, followed by test marketing.
3 As you requested, we have designed a campaign for launching your new 'Superchrom' cassettes.
4 We have had some new promotional literature printed giving full details of our products.
5 Experience here has shown that television advertising at peak periods may result in a 40% increase in sales.
6 Direct mail advertising means an improvement of the turnover that justifies the expenses.
7 Come to our showrooms next Wednesday for a preview of the coats. You will then benefit from the special reduction of 10%.
8 We look forward to seeing you at our store to make use of this attractive offer.
9 There's special discount on any orders that reach us by April 30.
10 Read the enclosed catalogue: you won't regret it.

Sentences for translation

1. Eine gute Werbekampagne basiert auf einer geschickten Kombination der Medien.
2. Verkäufe können durch einen Vertreter gefördert werden, der Kaufinteressenten und bestehende Kunden regelmässig besucht.
3. Wir finden, Ihre Werbekampagne ist gut geplant; da aber der Voranschlag ziemlich hoch ist, würden wir gerne die Kosten mit Ihnen besprechen.
4. Die landesweite Pressewerbung wird im März beginnen, gefolgt von der Verteilung von Flugblättern mit einem Wettbewerb für Kinder.
5. Die Reaktion [= Antwort] auf unsere Umfrage war enttäuschend und zeigte Vorlieben der Verbraucher nicht klar.
6. Ich stelle Ihnen gesondert etwas Werbematerial zu, das für Ihre Schaufenster und an Ausstellungen benutzt werden kann.

7. Wir schlagen vor, die Kampagne mit einer Anzahl Werbesendungen im Fernsehen zu eröffnen.
8. Unser Werbeleiter ist überzeugt, dass wiederholtes Zeitungswerben eine befriedigende Umsatzsteigerung hervorbringen [= produzieren] kann.
9. Die Handelsabteilung des Britischen Konsulats und die Handelskammer von Hongkong haben die Ehre, Sie zum Besuch der Ausstellung der neuesten Produkte der Hongkonger Industrie einzuladen.

Letters for translation

Von: EMCO Inc., Vancouver, Canada
An: Mr. Hal Hutcheson, 14 Main Street, Montreal, Canada
2. Februar 19..

Sehr geehrter Herr Hutcheson

Besten Dank für Ihren Brief vom 28. Januar, dem ein Entwurf des Werbeplans für Herbst und Winter beilag. Wir haben nun die Einzelheiten sorgfältig durchgesehen und stimmen mit Ihren Vorschlägen überein. Der Kostenvoranschlag steht in Übereinstimmung mit dem Ihnen vorgelegten Budget und lässt einen ausreichenden Betrag für Verkaufsbriefe und Auslagenmaterial übrig.
Wie von Ihnen vorgesehen, sollte jetzt Platz in Zeitungen und Zeitschriften gemäss Seite 2 Ihres Planes reserviert [= gebucht] werden, und wir hätten gerne, dass Sie dies ohne Verzögerung erledigen.

                Mit freundlichen Grüssen

Letter writing assignments

Schreiben Sie einen zügigen «Promotion»-Brief für dieses Buch «Dear Sirs».

21 Banking and payments

The word 'bank' comes from the Italian word 'banco', which means a little table. The money-lenders of Lombardy used these tables when they carried on their banking business in the Middle Ages.
Nowadays clients use banks for their money matters in many ways:

Savings and investments
Savings accounts can be opened with only a small amount. Money may be withdrawn immediately when it is needed.
Deposit accounts have a higher rate of interest, but a month's notice has to be given for withdrawals over a certain amount.
Long-term savings (which may be combined with life insurance) produce a substantial yield over the years.
Then there are investment plans, whereby a regular sum is put aside for the purchase of unit trusts or shares. They are an attractive way to build up a capital.

Borrowing money
House owners can borrow money at a fixed rate of interest to build or buy their home, for building extensions and making improvements.
Personal loans are available for almost any purpose and are repayable in monthly instalments over an agreed period.
Business loans often provide a flexible form of credit, enabling customers to acquire machines for instance, or to bridge the gap between making a purchase and the payment, which may result in better terms for the buyer.
An overdraft can be granted to current account holders if there is a suitable security.

Payments and receiving money
To save time going to the bank and to avoid the risk of carrying cash, there are convenient methods of making transfers.
A current account (Am. checking account) is the best one for receiving salary payments and making frequent payments by cheque or by bank transfer. Clients receive statements at certain periods showing transactions in and out of the account.
When foreign payments are made on credit the most important instruments are the draft or Bill of Exchange and the Documentary Letter of Credit. They allow the buyer a period of time in which to make the payment, and at the same time ensure the seller that the sum due will be payable on a specified date. The documentary credit is opened by the importer in favour of the exporter, and paid to him at his own bank in exchange for the shipping documents enabling the importer to collect the goods bought.

Banks' cheque cards, credit cards, cash cards
It is clear why these plastic cards are becoming more and more popular. Holders are able to pay for goods and services by cheque or on credit, and can obtain money from a cash dispenser day and night from their own bank.

Other banking services

These services include financial advice on all matters: tax problems, insurance, inheritances. For journeys abroad banks provide foreign currency and travellers cheques. They issue commercial bulletins and statistics, and supply information on a businessman's standing and solvency. Clients who keep their securities at the bank are relieved of all the administration involved, such as dividend and coupon collection, bond repayments and capital changes. Investment counselling and stock purchase are other services provided by banks for clients who want to buy securities on the stock exchange: stocks, shares and bonds. Valuables, gold bars and important documents may be safely stored in the banks' safes.

Businessmen can make payments at home and abroad by cheque. A banker's transfer or a SWIFT transfer (by telex) is another simple method of making payments abroad. By using a form the debtor instructs his bank to transfer a certain amount to the creditor at his local bank in the currency requested.

Cheque payment and clearance

Mr John Smith, who has a current account at Lloyds Bank, Europe Limited in London, sends a cheque for £112.16 to Mr George Marley, who banks with the Midland Bank in Malta. On receiving it, the Malta branch forwards Mr Smith's cheque to its head office in London. The following day at the Clearing House along with many other cheques, it is presented to Lloyds Bank's representatives for settlement to be made between the banks. Within the next day or so Mr Smith's bank will receive his cheque back and the amount in question will be withdrawn from his current account.

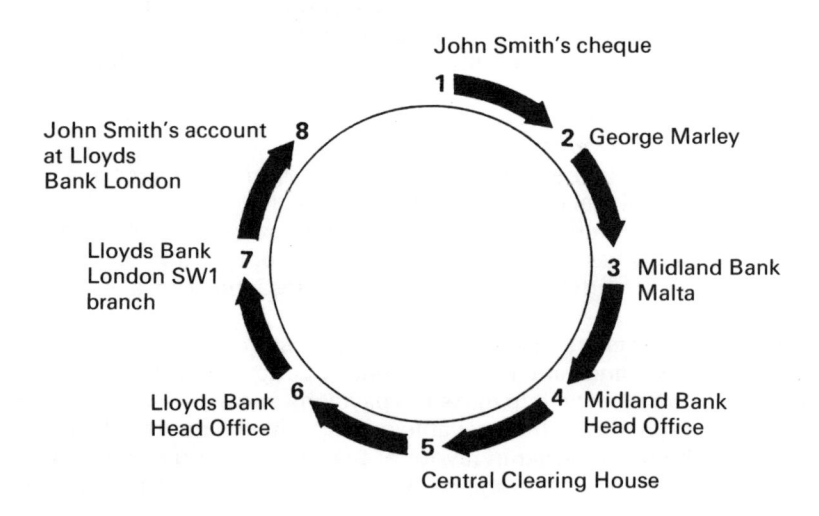

1. John Smith's cheque
2. George Marley
3. Midland Bank Malta
4. Midland Bank Head Office
5. Central Clearing House
6. Lloyds Bank Head Office
7. Lloyds Bank London SW1 branch
8. John Smith's account at Lloyds Bank London

money-lender	Geldverleiher
savings	Spargeld, Ersparnis
investment	Investition
withdraw, to	abheben
savings account	Sparkonto, Sparguthaben

deposit account	Depositenkonto
notice	hier: Kündigung
yield	Ertrag, Rendite
share	Anteil, Aktie
loan	Kredit
repayable	rückzahlbar
security	Sicherheit
overdraft	Überziehung
transfer	Überweisung
transaction	(Geschäfts)abschluss, geschäftl. Unternehmen
(documentary) letter of credit	Akkreditiv
cash dispenser	Bargeldautomat
tax	Steuer
inheritance	Erbschaft
currency	Währung
solvency	Zahlungsfähigkeit
securities	Effekten, Wertschriften
collection	Inkasso, Einziehung
bond	Obligation
investment counselling	Anlageberatung
stocks	Aktien, Wertpapiere
valuables	Wertsachen
gold bar	Goldbarren
creditor	Gläubiger
Clearing House	Verrechnungsstelle

Vocabulary exercise

Choose the correct words from the list.
1. Money lenders used to ___ ___ their transactions at small tables.
2. Customers can ___ their savings without notice from a ___ account.
3. Deposit accounts earn higher ___ but larger withdrawals cannot be made unless a month's ___ is given.
4. People who make savings for a longer time will get a better ___.
5. Regular savings can form a ___ when used to ___ unit trusts.
6. House ___ can use the house they are building as a security for a ___.
7. Money needed for ___ loans is usually repaid in monthly ___.
8. Cheque payments can be made by clients who have a ___ account.
9. Settlement between banks is made at a ___ house.
10. When making a SWIFT transfer, the debtor ___ his bank to send the amount due to the ___ bank.
11. The bill of ___ is an important document for ___ payments.
12. With a cash card bank customers can get cash from a ___ at any time.

capital
carry on
clearing
creditor's
current
dispenser
exchange
foreign
instalments
instructs
interest
loan
notice
owners
personal
pruchase
savings
withdraw
yield

ABC Bank Ltd
12 Coronation Street   Liverpool L1V 4PT

Carson City National Bank
173 10th Avenue
Carson City, Calif 90712
USA   June 17, 19..

Gentlemen:

By order of	Institute of Technology, Liverpool
we request you to open	an irrevocable letter of credit by air mail
for the amount of	US $5,270.00
currency	US dollars available to beneficiary
valid until	June 29, 19..
in favour of	Electronics Associates Inc (payee) Carson City, California
covering shipment of	P-60 electronic computer, Order No 47.34
available against the	5 commercial invoices 2 consular invoices certificate of insurance for $6,000.00 set of clean 'on board' bills of lading in duplicate
Special instructions	Documents to be airmailed to us

                                            Very truly yours

                                            ABC Bank Ltd
                                            Liverpool

LITTONS BANK LTD
34 Pembroke Street
Leeds LE4 1AD

R P Murray Esq
"Hillside"
Ridgeway Crescent
Leeds LE6 2BG   16 November 19..

Dear Mr Murray

It was a pleasure meeting you at our offices last week and discussing with you the investment of your assets, amounting to approximately £10,000. As the amount is at present on a current account, it bears only very little interest. The proceeds you would obtain from a deposit account (up to the amount of £2,000) are less than 5% per annum.

After referring the matter to our Head Office investment counselling service, we would recommend your investing part of the sum in stocks and shares of reputable companies, likely to provide favourable dividends and offering the probability of capital appreciation. Investment of another part in bonds would provide a reasonable yield and offer the advantage of prices less influenced by market fluctuations, and a fixed rate of interest.

We are enclosing a number of prospectuses, describing new issues of public and company loans, together with a proposal for investing your assets. Our bank is in a position to purchase any of these, or other securities at short notice, crediting your account with the proceeds, dealing with coupon collection and representing you at shareholders' meetings.

We should be pleased to advise you further if you require any other particulars or proposals.

                              Yours truly

beneficiary	*Begünstigter*
in duplicate	*im Doppel*
assets	*Aktiva*
per annum	*pro Jahr*
capital appreciation	*Kapitalzuwachs*
fluctuation	*Schwankung*

Model sentences (banking and payments)

1 Please use the enclosed crossed cheque for £200 to open a joint current account on 1 January 19.. in the names of Joan Sanders and Martin Sanders. We enclose the card you submitted to us with our specimen signatures.
2 As soon as we receive confirmation that the credit has been opened, the goods will be shipped and the documents presented for clearance at the bank.
3 Our bank, The Commonwealth Bank of Canada, has been instructed to make a telex transfer of the amount in settlement of your pro forma invoice No. BD/71.
4 Please note that we have requested the Northerland Bank of Liverpool to open an irrevocable letter of credit for £1040 in your favour. You will receive confirmation from our agents, Messrs Reed & Sons.
5 We would like to know the present rate of interest on a deposit account, and what minimum balance is required in a current account.
6 Please purchase the following foreign currency at the best possible rate of exchange, and debit my current account.
7 Thank you for the advice your gave me when I spoke to Mr H. J. Hanwell of your consulting service. I have decided to follow your recommendations and invest the balance of my account accordingly.
8 In view of the present trends on the stock market, we would like to sell the holdings detailed below, and to invest the amount realized in life insurance.

Sentences for translation

1. Bitte geben Sie uns alle Wirtschaftsbulletins, die Sie über den Handel in Malaysia vorrätig haben.
2. Wir erbitten eine Bankauskunft über Herrn J. Moncrief aus Inverness, seine Vermögenslage und Zahlungsfähigkeit betreffend.
3. Würden Sie für uns bitte fremde Währung gemäss beigefügter Aufstellung kaufen und unser Konto Nr. 16-310 (entsprechend) belasten.
4. Wir bitten Sie, ein unwiderrufliches Akkreditiv per Luftpost über den Betrag von 3,200 Dollar zu eröffnen, gültig bis zum 31. Dezember 19.. zu Gunsten der Shell Petroleum Company.
5. Ich lege einen auf mich gezogenen, akzeptierten Wechsel der Gebrüder Senn

aus München bei und wäre froh, die Dokumente für die fraglichen Waren zu erhalten.
6. In Anbetracht des Saldos auf meinem Kontokorrent und des höheren Zinssatzes auf Depositenkonten, würde ich gerne mittels Überweisung von £ 500 von meinem Konto Nr. C40-923 ein Depositenkonto auf meinen Namen eröffnen.
7. Wir empfehlen Ihnen, sich an unsere Anlageabteilung zu wenden. Sie werden in der Lage sein, einen Vorschlag über den Kauf von Aktien und Obligationen zu machen, die einen vernünftigen Ertrag abwerfen.
8. Unsere Bank kann jede dieser Wertschriften für Sie besorgen, Coupon-Inkasso vornehmen und Ihrem Konto Verkäufe und Dividenden gutschreiben.

Letters for translation

1. Von: Walkwell Footwear PLC, Northampton N19 3AF
   An: Midland Bank, Northampton N18 2BF

   3. November 19..

   Sehr geehrte Herren

   Wir senden Ihnen hiermit die beiliegenden Verschiffungspapiere, die die Schuh- und Stiefelsendung für die Firma:

   Smart & Bossman
   Nr. Clock Gate
   Montreal, Canada

   im Werte von £ 8,020 betreffen.
   Die Dokumente sind dem Schuldner auszuhändigen, nachdem er die beigelegte Tratte unterschrieben hat. Der Wechsel ist 90 Tage nach Sicht fällig. Bitte veranlassen Sie, dass die Commenwealth Bank von Kanada das Akzept verschafft und den Wechsel bei Verfall zur Zahlung vorweist.

   Mit freundlichen Grüssen

   Beilagen:
   Wechsel
   Schiffsfrachtbrief
   Versicherungspolice
   Handelsfakturen
   Konsulatsfakturen

2. Von: Allgemeine Hypothekarbank, 3000 Bern
   An: International Bank for Reconstruction & Development, Washington, D.C. 20013

   10. April 19..

Wir haben von der Britischen Handelskommission in Colombo erfahren, dass in Sri Lanka ein grosses Bauprogramm für Touristenhotels besteht [= ist]. Man erwartet, dass Sri Lanka mit seiner günstigen geografischen Lage ein beliebtes Ferienzentrum werden wird.

Um das Projekt zu finanzieren, werden ca. 18 Millionen Schweizer Franken notwendig sein. Ein Zehntel dieser Summe wird von lokalen Geldgebern zur Verfügung gestellt. Ein zweiter Betrag – von noch unbekannter Höhe – darf von einer Britischen Finanzgesellschaft erwartet werden. Wir sind angefragt worden, 10 Millionen Franken in dieses Bauprogramm zu investieren. Wir alleine können einen solch hohen Betrag nicht gewähren; die angebotenen Sicherheiten erscheinen uns ungenügend. Darum leiten wir das Gesuch zur wohlwollenden Prüfung an Sie weiter.

Mit freundlichen Grüssen

Letter writing assignments

The Egyptian Hotel Suppliers Ltd, 62 Sharif Street, Cairo, Egypt, hat bei Ihnen elektrische Wärmeplatten im Wert von £ 10,800 bestellt. Die Firma möchte nach Erhalt der Ware mit einem Verrechnungscheck bezahlen. Antworten Sie, indem Sie auf die Zahlungsbedingungen verweisen, die ein Akkreditiv verlangen.

22 Applications

> We have a challenging opening for a young
>
> ## INTERNAL AUDITOR
>
> (Betriebswirtschafter lic. oec./Betriebsökonom HWV/HSG – degree in business economics or overseas equivalent) to enter our Internal Audit Department.
>
> He will work in a team on preparing and carrying out audits in affiliates, to ensure compliance with Group internal instructions and to complement the work of external auditors.
>
> Audit results are discussed with local management and presented to Group manangement in a specific report.
>
> The ideal candidate will have had some years' experience in a similar activity. He should be capable of working both independently and in a team as well as having an analytical approach and an ability to work effectively with all levels of management.
>
> Ability to communicate well in English – both verbally and in writing – is essential, and a good knowledge of at least one of the following languages – Italian, French or Spanish – would be an asset. Frequent overseas travel will be included.
>
> Applications, with a full c. v., in English, should be sent to

> SECRETARY, experienced and capable of working on own initiative urgently required for office manager. Applicant should have good knowledge of English, German and French. Beginning salary according to experience. Apply to Box AI 8193, "Neue Zürcher Zeitung."

These job advertisements in English call for applications written in English. The advertiser may want to see how the prospective employee writes a letter in this language. In any case, a written application carries more weight than does a phone call and is likely to be taken seriously.

If the applicant has had only one job, this can be described in the letter, but where experience is more varied it is better to enclose a data sheet (or curriculum vitae) describing education, past jobs and qualifications. Be careful in writing these neatly and correctly; it is worth taking trouble for the position you want to get. Write facts which the employer wants to know for the vacancy in question, pointing out the abilities you can offer that makes you suitable for the job.

apply, to	*sich bewerben*
applicant	*Bewerber*
application	*Bewerbung*

advertise, to		inserieren
advertiser		Inserent
advertisement		Inserat
carry weight, to		hier: grössere Bedeutung zukommen
experience		Erfahrung
varied		vielfältig
data sheet		
curriculum vitae (cv)		Lebenslauf
resumé		
neat		ordentlich, übersichtlich
it is worth ... ing		es lohnt sich zu ...
ability		Fähigkeit

Stelle, Stellung	position
	job (conversational)
	situation (especially domestic and when listed in newspapers)
	post (a higher or official position)
	employment
offene Stelle	vacancy

Zeugnis	testimonial	Empfehlungsschreiben
	certificate	Fähigkeitszeugnis

Vocabulary exercise

Complete these sentences with words from the list.

1 A ____ employee who is looking for a ____ should write the ____ in English if the advertisement is in English.
2 Perhaps the ____ wants to see how well the ____ can write a ____ in this language.
3 Sometimes only a letter is ____ in answer to a job ____, but if the person concerned has varied ____, an enclosed data sheet is ____.
4 ____ should be taken in writing such a letter, because the applicant's whole ____ could depend on it.
5 So it is ____ taking enough ____ when describing your ____.
6 I am accustomed to ____ most of the work on my ____.
7 In my last job I was present at ____ meetings to take ____ notes.
8 Afterwards I typed the ____ for my employer to sign.
9 Enclosed is a ____ sheet, giving you all the ____ of previous jobs.
10 I do hope you will ____ me, so that I may come for an ____.

advertisement
applicant
application
better
board
care
contact
data
doing
employer
experience
future
interview
job
letter
minutes
own
particulars
prospective
qualifications
shorthand
trouble
worth
written

170

Rosmarie Halder
Rasenstrasse 39
6006 Lucerne

                                            The Advertiser
                                            Box No. AI 8193
                                            "Neue Zürcher Zeitung"
                                            8008 Zurich

                                            19 March 19..

Dear Sirs

The "Neue Zürcher Zeitung" of today's date advertises that you urgently require an experienced secretary. I feel sure that my qualifications will meet your needs; moreover, I should be free to commence work at the beginning of next month.

As you will note from the enclosed testimonial copies, I am accustomed to working independently. My last employer gave me most of his routine correspondence to deal with myself. When he dictated the more complicated letters I could take shorthand at a speed of 120 words per minute. I was often present at board meetings, sales promotion planning, and so on, in order to take shorthand notes and type the minutes or reports afterwards.

After a good educational grounding I supplemented my school study of languages with special courses and residence abroad (a year in Bath, England and ten months in Paris), and now have acquired a good command of English and French. I hold the English language certificate of the British-Swiss Chamber of Commerce.

The attached Data Sheet will give you further particulars of my office experience. Of course, I shall be pleased to come for an interview at any time convenient to you and supply any further information personally. May I hear from you soon? My telephone number is 041 34 92 16.

                                            Yours faithfully

Enclosure

Peter Fischer
Lindenweg 14
8008 Zurich

The Advertiser
Box No. AI 8194
"Neue Zürcher Zeitung"
8008 Zurich

19th March, 19..

Dear Sirs

Vacancy for Internal Auditor

Your advertisement in today's "Neue Zürcher Zeitung" prompts me to apply for the position of internal auditor in your Company.

The enclosed curriculum vitae describes my education, experience and qualifications. From it you will see that in addition to office experience in banking as well as industry, I have taken several courses in various aspects of accountancy and recently returned from a two-year stay at Texas University where I successfully completed a MBA. Also enclosed are two copies of testimonials from previous employers.

Although my present position is a pleasant one, it offers no good prospects, and that is why I should prefer employment in an expanding organization like yours. May I request you not to contact my employer for the time being, as I have not yet given notice.

If my qualifications interest you, I should appreciate the opportunity of meeting you.

Yours faithfully

Enclosures: Curriculum vitae
2 copies of testimonials

CURRICULUM VITAE

Personal details

Name: Peter Fischer   Date of birth: 14.2...
Address: Lindenweg 14, 8008 Zurich   Marital Status: Single

Education

1966-72   Primary School, Baden
1972-75   Secondary School, Baden
1975-78   Swiss Mercantile College, Baden
1982-84   Master of Business Administration,
          University of Texas, U.S.A.

Business Experience

1975-78   Union Bank of Switzerland,
              Baden   Business trainee
1979-82   Messrs. Brown Boveri, Ltd.
              Baden, Costing Department   Bookkeeping assistant
since 1985   Messrs. Ramsayer & Co.,
              Exporters, Zurich   Internal Auditor

References

Dr. G. Fister, Bank Manager, Union Bank of Switzerland, Baden
Mr. H. Gretener, Bookkeeper, BBC, Baden

vacancy	*offene Stelle*
initiative	*Initiative*
require, to	*suchen*
knowledge	*Kenntnis*
salary	*Gehalt, Salär*
box	*Chiffre*
expand, to	*(sich) ausdehnen*
expanding	*entwicklungsfähig*
position, post	*Stelle*
promotion	*Beförderung, Aufstieg*
particulars	*Angaben, Einzelheiten*
qualification	*Fähigkeit*
testimonial	*Zeugnis*
accustom (to), to	*gewöhnen (an)*
independent	*selbständig*
speed	*Geschwindigkeit*
present	*anwesend*
minutes (pl.)	*Protokoll*
education	*Ausbildung, Erziehung*
educational to supplement	*Bildungsergänzen*
course	*Kurs*
residence	*Aufenthalt*
command	*Beherrschung*
certificate	*Zeugnis*
interview	*Unterredung*
prompt, to	*bewegen zu, veranlassen*
banking	*Bankwesen*
industry	*Industrie*
accountancy	*Rechnungswesen, Buchführung*
relevant	*entsprechend, einschlägig*
employer	*Arbeitgeber*
employment	*Stellung, Beschäftigung*
prospect	*Aussicht*
contact, to	*in Verbindung treten mit*

Model sentences (applications)

1. Your advertisement states that you require a personal assistant to the managing director.
2. I am very interested in the secretarial position advertised in yesterday's paper.
3. Although I have not yet had much experience in this field, I feel sure that the work is suitable for someone with my abilities.
4. In my present job I was trained in the use of a word processor, and can also write simple programmed correspondence.
5. After completing my studies at the XY School, I went abroad to improve my knowledge of languages.
6. Would you let me know when it would be convenient for me to come to your office for a personal meeting.
7. My present employer will write a testimonial, describing my abilities and character.

8 As far as salary is concerned, I would prefer to discuss this with you at a interview.
9 My present earnings are Sfr... per annum.
10 The two companies will be merging at the end of the year, that is why I am looking for a new position.

```
personnel   Personal
personal    persönlich
```

Sentences for translation

1. Unter Bezugnahme auf Ihr Inserat in der Schweizerischen Kaufmännischen Zeitung vom 12. Februar möchte ich mich für die Stelle eines Computer-Programmierers in Ihrer Firma bewerben.
2. Die inserierte Stelle entspricht genau meinen Fähigkeiten.
3. Der Grund, weshalb ich meine Stelle wechsle, ist der, dass ich es vorziehe, mehr Arbeit mit Eigeninitiative zu verrichten.
4. Wie Sie aus dem beigelegten Lebenslauf entnehmen können, habe ich Verkaufserfahrung in Büromaschinen.
5. Bitte entnehmen Sie weitere Einzelheiten aus dem beigefügten Lebenslauf.
6. Ich habe Kurse in Datenverarbeitung und Betriebswirtschaftslehre besucht.
7. Der Zweijahreskurs für zweisprachige Sekretärinnen wird nächsten Monat beendet sein; so wäre ich in der Lage, eine neue Stelle am 1. November anzutreten.
8. Falls Sie wünschen, dass ich zu einem Interview in Ihr Büro kommen soll, lassen Sie mich bitte wissen, wann es Ihnen passen würde.

Letters for translation

1. Von: Albert Bond & Co., Rüdenstrasse 25, 4000 Düsseldorf 1
   An: Inseratenabteilung, Daily Telegraph, London EC4

   9. Januar 19..

   Wir bitten Sie, das folgende Inserat zweispaltig in Ihrer Zeitung vom 17. und 22. Januar 19.. zu plazieren:

   Amerikanisches Unternehmen, das seinen europäischen Geschäft(sbe-reich) in Deutschland ausdehnt,
   sucht tüchtige Sekretärin
   für allgemeine Büroarbeiten, einschliesslich Korrespondenz in Englisch, Französisch und Deutsch nach Diktat.

Bewerbungen mit Angaben über Ausbildung und Fähigkeiten sind zu richten an Chiffre ... «Daily Telegraph»

Bitte schicken Sie uns Ihre Rechnung bis zum 25. Januar samt den entsprechenden Exemplaren Ihrer Zeitung.

Mit freundlichem Gruss

2. Von: Peter Schwarz, Hügelstrasse 105, 4600 Olten
An: The United Book Corporation, rue du Prieuré, 1200 Genève

10. Januar 19..

Sehr geehrte Herren

An der kürzlichen Versammlung des Schweizerischen Buchhändler- und Verlegervereins hat Ihr Prokurist, Herr Daniel Huber, darauf hingewiesen, dass Sie einen Angestellten für die Buchhaltungsabteilung suchen.
Während des letzten Jahres habe ich die ganze Buchhaltung meines Arbeitgebers selbständig besorgt [done] sowie einen Teil der Kundenkorrespondenz. Ich wünsche meine jetzige Stelle zu verlassen, um Berufserfahrungen in einem grösseren Betrieb zu erwerben.
Der beigelegte Lebenslauf enthält genaue Einzelheiten über meinen Bildungsgang und meine Fähigkeiten.
Sofern Ihnen meine Bewerbung zusagt, bin ich gerne bereit, zu einer persönlichen Unterredung nach Genf zu kommen.
Sollten Sie mich als Ihren Mitarbeiter anstellen, kann ich Ihnen sorgfältiges und zuverlässiges Arbeiten zusichern.

Mit freundlichen Grüssen

Beilagen:
Lebenslauf
Zeugniskopien
Fähigkeitsausweis der Lehrabschlussprüfung

23 Remarks on Grammar & Style

A. How to bring good style into letter writing

Here is a letter which was written by a new sales assistant, when he was asked to acknowledge receipt of an order. Although most accessories were available, a few could only be supplied later.

Dear Sirs
We acknowledge receipt of you order of 8 March. We have all the parts ordered in stock except ...
We hope to have this accessory available within four weeks. We cannot avoid the delay ...

Although this letter was correct as far as language was concerned (grammar, spelling, etc), the style should be improved. In this letter all the sentences start with "we". It is better not to use "we" or "I" so much as it makes the writer sound self-important. The length of the sentences should be varied: some can be short, others longer. Unless the letter is an extremely short one, it should contain two or more paragraphs: this is easier to read than one solid block of text and notes can be written in. It would be good to add a sentence with a sales message and to make the whole letter sound friendlier and pleasanter to read.

Exercise: Rewrite this letter in the way suggested.

Dealing with complaints

When dealing with complaints, make a point of telling the customer what is being done to put matters right. In case of a delay he wants to know when delivery can be expected. Where goods have been damaged in transit he must be informed whether and how he will be compensated. Think the 5 c's of letter writing.

1 Clear
2 Courteous
3 Concise
4 Co-operative
5 Complete

and to write a good letter you should bear them in mind. Courtesy, especially, is required when dealing with complaints:

It is better to say:	Than:
We are sorry our price-list was not quite clear.	You must have misunderstood our price-list.
Your complaint has been thoroughly investigated and we suggest ...	We have never received complaints of this kind before.
Please give us another opportunity of rectifying the impression you received from this unfortunate occurrence.	As you are so dissatisfied with our service, we suggest you take your business elsewhere in the future.
We apologize for the error and enclose our rectified invoice.	The error was made by our invoice typist.
In order to avoid a misunderstanding in future, we shall ask you for packing instructions in advance.	You are wrong; you did not let us have your packing instructions in time.
Your claim has been passed on to our insurance company who will get into touch with you soon.	We regret that we cannot give your any better news.

The You attitude

Another way of making your letters more courteous and cooperative is to take into account the YOU attitude. This means bringing in the word "you" more than "I" or "we", and can generally be done in these ways:

- psychologically
  - by thinking of the reader's interests and writing about them (see examples 1, 2, 3 below);
- positively
  - telling your reader what can be done, and not what cannot be done (examples 4, 5);
- in language
  - avoiding the use of "I" and "we" by writing "you" or by using a passive, an imperative construction or a question (other examples)

It is better to say: (YOU attitude)	Than: (I attitude)
1 Your advertisement calls for a shorthand typist or dictaphone typist.	I wish to offer myself for the position of shorthand typist.
2 The knowledge and experience I can offer you are ...	I am looking for a job where I can ...
3 This special offer of raw material will save you money.	This is the cheapest raw material we can offer.

4 Your request of 5 June has been passed on to our head office. You will be hearing from them shortly.	As we told you in our last letter, we cannot give you the information wanted.
5 Although there has been an increase this month, you will find that the prices are still quite competitive.	We cannot, unfortunately, quote the same prices as last month, although they are still quite competitive.
6 Please remember that ...	We must point out that ...
7 A delay in delivery would have caused my customers to be disappointed.	I would have disappointed my customers if I had allowed a delay in delivery.
8 You can now enjoy the convenience of buying by mail.	We are pleased to announce our new "Buy by mail" service.
9 You and other dealers like you bought 10,000 of these cars last year.	We sold over 10,000 of these cars last year.
10 May we invite you to see the typewriters in our showrooms?	We can demonstrate the typewriters in our showrooms.
11 Please ask Mr. Edwards to sign the policy.	We must have the policyholder's signature.

B. Division of words, display of a letter text

A well displayed text of a letter looks attractive if it has a fairly balanced appearance, ie if the left-hand margins are regular and the right-hand margins as regular as possible.
On the whole, English words are short, but there are longer ones that you may have to divide. As a division is a disturbance to the reader, you should give her or him as much help as possible on the first line – so that the word can almost be guessed – and put a suffix or the shorter part on the next line.

Rules

1 Keep the root of the word intact, dividing prefixes or suffixes:
contra-dict, assist-ance, divi-sion, con-firm-a-tion

2 Words are usually divided between doubled consonants:
mes-sage, cot-ton, recom-mend, mil-lion, pos-si-bil-ity

but if the original word ends in a double letter, follow rule 1:
fill-ing, agree-ment, busi-ness-man

3 Divide between syllables
(see English dictionary):
prob-ably, morn-ing, occa-sion, fa-cil-i-tate, sec-re-tary, spe-cial

4 Do *not* divide short words, or words of one syllable:
money, water, only; straight, breathe, through

Do not divide for one or two letters; do not divide contractions or abbreviations:
ended, dirty, against; shouldn't, haven't

5 Names, figures and amounts should not be divided:
Mr J B Martin   £14.12 p   4.20 p.m.

Exercise

Indicate if and where these words should be divided

holidays   appearance
development   application
television   comfortable
qualifications   latest
transport   acknowledge
carriage   cheque
agency   opinion
                  realize

C. Punctuation

When used	Example

■ FULL STOP (AM. PERIOD)

1 To end sentences.   Thank you for your letter.
2 At the end of abbreviations (Especially American)   U.S.A. dept.
3 As a decimal point.   98.4°, $17.70

? QUESTION MARK

At the end of a question.   Have the goods arrived yet?
(Not generally used after a request: Will you please reply as soon as possible.)

! EXCLAMATION MARK

Only after an exclamation.   Oh, no! It can't be true!
(Not normally used in business correspondence. Should not be used too often in English.)

: COLON

1 To confirm or extend meaning of previous statement.   Give advice in private: advice given in public is not likely to be accepted.
2 Preceding a list, enumeration or quotation.   Please deliver the following:
                                                            Four colours are available: green, grey, black and blue.
3 After salutation, U.S.A.   Dear Mr. Clark:

; SEMICOLON

1. For a pause longer than a comma.
2. For two connected (or contrasting) ideas.

Would you mind looking into the matter; there must have been a misunderstanding.

, COMMA

1. To separate a series of nouns, adjectives, adverbs, etc.
   The gloves are available in small, medium (,) * or large sizes.
2. Before a conjunction in a long, compound sentence (pause). *
   We have never traded with Canada in the past, but we may start next year.
3. A name, or description in apposition.
   We have asked our traveller, Mr. Robinson, to call on you.
4. To separate phrases or clauses only if they could possibly be removed.

   Necessary clause (restrictive)
   A car that has been repaired properly is as good as new.
   If I see you next week I shall give it to you.

   Removable clause (non-restrictive)
   The car, which had been repaired three times already, was out of order again.
   I shall give it to you next week, or, if that is impossible, send it to you.

5. To separate thousands in numbers.
   15,000,000   £ 2,019.60 p
6. In addresses between city and state in dates (American)
   Chicago, Illinois 60611
   March 6, 1986
7. Before direct speech; to introduce a quotation; after salutation and complimentary close.
   In opening his speech, the chairman said, "Ladies and Gentlemen, ..."
8. If a pause is indicated, especially before and after these words: *
   actually, after all, anyway, apparently, as a matter of fact, besides, by the way, consequently, finally, for example, for instance, fortunately, further, furthermore, however, in addition, in any case, in fact, in the meantime, meanwhile, moreover, namely (viz.), nevertheless, no, no doubt, normally, obviously, of course, on the other hand, naturally, perhaps, personally, that is (i. e.), therefore, to tell the truth, unfortunately, well, yes.
9. When participial or infinitive phrase precedes main clause. *
   Knowing the difficulties, I cannot recommend this action.
10. **Compared with German** no comma is needed before clauses starting with:
    that, until,
    if, whether, while;
    indirect speech, indirect answers;
    infintive and participle constructions;
    before and after necessary relative clauses;

    I knew that he would come.
    Mr. Jones asked if the mail was ready.
    They told me it was all right.
    The manager agreed to raise my salary.
    Is this everything we need to know about commas?

* Comma optional

If in doubt leave the comma out.

( ) BRACKETS (AM. PARENTHESES)

To enclose remarks, explanation or reference.
Next year (1972) we can raise our turnover.

" "
QUOTATION MARKS (INVERTED COMMAS)

1. For direct quotations. — "We are glad," the letter began, "that you wrote to us immediately."
2. For titles, names, headings quoted. — The title of the article is "Advertising in Africa."

' SINGLE QUOTATION MARKS

For a quotation within a quotation. — The last sentence of the memorandum ran, "Please write, 'Paid' and your initials at the bottom of each invoice."

— HYPHEN

1. Parts of a compound adjective. — a first-class compartment (but: He is in the first class); up-to-date styles; a 20-year-old stamp; the above-mentioned item, non-returnable.
2. A compound noun. — brother-in-law (but no hyphen is needed in well-established compounds: (bathroom, schoolboy, semicolon)

   Parts of numbers. — twenty-four, two and three-quarters
3. A title representing two officers (and often in a two-word title): — Secretary-Treasurer, Vice-President, ex-editor

— DASH

1. To indicate interrupted thought. — "If I get hold of you, I'll—" she did not finish.
2. For special emphasis. — The office was complete except for one thing—a desk.
3. As brackets. — It was the manager—not the programmer—who made the mistake.

' APOSTROPHE

1. For possessive of nouns. — A week's salary, the companies' profits.
2. Omission of letters and figures. — Can't (cannot), it's (it is, it has), rec'd (received), The' 20s.
3. Plurals of numbers, letters, words and signs. — Do not use &'s instead of and's in a letter. In the 1970's.

D. How to write numbers

Large numbers or amounts	30,000 or 30 000	5 million or 5 m	$12 000
	(do not use abbrevious for thousand or hundreds)		
Amounts	£17.20 $31.50 $4.75 (Put a decimal point before pence and cents)		
Small amounts	20 c 50 p $0.95 0.30		
Round numbers	$20.00 or $20 £100		
Decimals	2.5% 98.4°F (degrees Fahrenheit)		

> billion (U.S.A.) = 1000 million
> = Milliarde

Use words

Small numbers (up to 10 or 12):
I have had four years' experience.
Of the three houses only one was vacant.
Fifth Avenue

Approximate or round figures:
We received about fifty applications.
There are five thousand people.
We saw more than fifteen hundred wild animals (preferred to "one thousand five hundred")

At the beginning of sentences:
Twenty-six representatives sell our products.

Fractions alone:
About one third of the building was occupied.

Centures and decades:
The thirtieth anniversary
In the nineteenth century

In certain legal documents:
... is valid from the fifteenth of March
Pay twenty-six pounds tenpence ...

Time:
It is ten o'clock.
He has lunch at half past twelve every day (Conversational style).

Note two hundred members, hundreds of members
twenty million inhabitants, many millions of inhabitants

Use figures

When writing in list form:
We need 6 pencils, 2 erasers and 1 box of paper clips

For more than two or three words:
350

Weights, measures, abbreviations and signs:
5 lb   10 gallons   5%

Large numbers:
12 000 000 or 12 million   2 billion

Mixed fractions:
2¾   12½

Time:
Office hours are from 9 a.m. to 5.30 p.m.
He has lunch at 12.30 p.m. every day
The museum is open from 09.00–17.00 daily except Mondays (official style)

It is clearer to write	than
In the year 1983 there were 4,902 people who moved out of town.	In the year 1983 4,902 people moved out of town.
Cut it into fifteen 20-inch strips.	Cut it into 15 20-inch strips.
Would you get me four 10 p stamps, please.	Would you get me 4 10 p stamps, please.

E. Passive

The *Passive* is used far more in English than in German, mainly

1. when we are more concerned with the *thing* which is being dealt with than the person doing the action and
2. as a substitute for *man* in German.

It is used frequently in business letters, reports and technical descriptions.

Be + Past Participle

The parcel is sent	Present	is/are
The parcel was sent	Past	was/were
The parcel has been sent	Perfect	has/have been
The parcel will be sent	Future	shall/will be
The parcel would be sent	Conditional	should/would be

must

The parcel must be sent	Present	must be	
The parcel had to be sent	Past	had to be	
The parcel will have to be sent	Future	will have to be	
The parcel has had to be sent	Perfect	has had to be	Past Participle

note also:
The parcel must have been sent

can

The parcel can be sent	Present	can be
The parcel could be sent	Past	could be
The parcel could have been sent	Perfect	could have been
The parcel is being sent	Present Cont.	is/are being
The parcel was being sent	Past Cont.	was/were being
... to the parcel being sent	Present Partic. Gerund	being

EXAMPLE *Diese Artikel können nicht verkauft werden*, *wenn sie zu teuer sind*.
These articles <u>cannot be sold</u> if they are too expensive.

VON/DURCH *Die Sendung wurde <u>von</u> der Polizei untersucht*.
The consignment was examined <u>by</u> the police.

MAN *<u>Man hat uns mitgeteilt</u>, dass die Preise herabgesetzt worden sind*.
<u>We have been</u> informed that the prices have been reduced.

MAN SAGT *<u>Man sagt (von ihm)</u>, er sei ein guter Geschäftsmann*.
<u>He is said to</u> be a good businessman.

Exercises
1 Rewrite in the passive
1 (We) *ship all our watches* by air freight.
2 The supplier *can dispatch the goods* on the 15 March.
3 Business friends *have informed us* that you can supply the deck chairs.
4 The price is subject to *(our) receiving your order* by the end of this week.
5 If (you) *entrust us* with a standing order, (we) *can reduce our prices* by 7½%.
6 *Have* (you) *included* carriage in your price?
7 Can (we) *supply the deck chairs* from stock?
8 The new range *will certainly interest him.*
9 The Snowsport Shoe Company *has* recently *appointed us* as agents.
10 They *make the shoes* of best quality leather.

2 Translate, using passive wherever possible
1. Sendungen werden mehr und mehr mit dem Flugzeug befördert [verschifft].
2. Sofortige Verschiffung wird verlangt.
3. Unsere Quittung vom 11. Juni liegt diesem Brief bei.
4. Man hat ihr (einen) höheren Lohn versprochen.
5. Die Artikel werden soeben in unserem Lagerhaus wieder verpackt.
6. Die Firma wurde vor zehn Jahren gegründet.
7. Man kann Waren frankiert oder unfrankiert senden.
8. Die Möbel werden Ihnen morgen geliefert werden.
9. Die Rechnung kann innert 30 Tagen bezahlt werden.
10. Ein Skonto kann nur bei Bestellung einer grösseren Menge gewährt werden.
11. Man erwartet nächstes Jahr viele Besucher an der "British Exhibition".
12. Die Preise können nicht ermässigt werden.
13. Diese Artikel werden bald ausverkauft sein.
14. Die Uhren werden versandt, sobald wir von unserer Bank die Bestätigung des Akkreditivs erhalten haben.
15. Die Kataloge und Preislisten für Detailhändler werden sofort abgeschickt.
16. Die Rechnung muss gestern abgesandt worden sein.
17. Warum sind diese Briefe noch nicht geöffnet worden?
18. Können Sie mir sagen, von wem diese Preise angegeben worden sind?
19. Beim Auspacken müssen alle Ersatzteile genau geprüft werden.
20. Man sagt, die neuen Büros seien sehr schön.
21. Die Bestellung wird zu Ihrer vollen Zufriedenheit ausgeführt werden.

F. Simple and continuous tenses

Simple

PRESENT

Repeated or habitual action:
We *revise* our price-lists yearly.

> never, sometimes, often, usually, always, if, as soon as, until

A general truth:
It *pays* to advertise.

PAST

Action completed in the past:
Why *did* you *buy* those cheap watches?
The offer *expired* last week.

PERFECT

Action which commenced in the past but continues to the present time.
Action just completed:
I *have finished* this work.

FUTURE

Action expressing future, willingness or promise:
We think he *will pay* the account by instalments.

Continuous (Progressive)

Action going on:
What *are* you *doing?* I *am writing* a letter.

> now, still, just or this meaning

Action in the near future or to express intention:
He *is arriving* tomorrow.
Are you *going* to remind the customers?

Action lasting for a certain time in the past:
I *was working* in the office when the phone rang.
While Miss Frank *was typing* Mr. Blackman *was checking* the cards.

Length of time is stressed:
We *have been waiting* for your confirmation.
Have you *been learning* English long?

Action going on during a certain time in the future:
The machine *will be working* by the time you come.

Note: Some verbs expressing thoughts, feelings and facts normally occur in *Simple* tenses:

> believe, belong, forget, hate, hear, know, like, love, mean, own, possess, prefer, remember, see, seem, suit, surprise, understand

Passive sentences follow similar rules (present and past continuous only):
The trade fair is *being organized* by the sales manager.
The goods *were being* checked when the discrepancy *was noticed*.

Exercise

Translate these sentences

1. Herr Rainer kommt morgen vormittag nach Zürich.

2. Ich habe die ganze Woche gearbeitet. Wenn Sie zurückkommen, werde ich noch an der Arbeit [Verb] sein.
3. Ich habe die Absicht, diese Prospekte als gewöhnliche Paketpost zu schicken.
4. Als ich in Frankreich wohnte, traf ich viele Amerikaner.
5. Gewöhnlich wohne ich in Deutschland, jetzt weile ich in der Schweiz.
6. Schreibst du immer englische Briefe? Nein, ich mache auch italienische und spanische Übersetzungen.
7. Ich kenne seine Adresse, aber ich kann (mich) jetzt nicht mehr daran erinnern.
8. Ich kann nicht kommen, ich telefoniere gerade.
9. Wir erwarten Ihre baldige Offerte.
10. Sobald ich Anweisungen von Herrn Blackman erhalte, versende ich die Ware.
11. Wo (hin) gehen Sie? Ich gehe ins Büro; ich gehe immer um diese Zeit.
12. Ich fand keine passende Stelle, obwohl ich schon seit vielen Monaten eine suche.
13. Während Herr Secrest telefonierte, schrieb Fräulein Miller nicht (auf der Maschine).
14. Was wirst du morgen um diese Zeit tun?
15. Dieser eingeschriebene Brief wird heute morgen abgeschickt [present continuous passive].

G. Past, Pluperfect, Perfect

The rules for expressing actions in the past in English are quite different from those in German.

PAST

1 An action completed in the past:

"*Did you see* Mr Blackman when you *went* to the warehouse?"—"Yes, I *met* his assistant too, Mr Foster."

2 An action in the past when the time is definite:

Thank you for your letter which we *received* yesterday. However, you *did not mention* the terms.

Past is often used with: yesterday, last week, on 4 Feb., when, ago

PERFECT

1 An action which started in the past, continuing to the present time:
Mr. Sigrist *has dealt* in office machines for fifty years and *had acquired* a good reputation.

2 An action in the past when the time is not definite:
I *have ordered* some more deck chairs, but prices *have risen* lately.

3 An action just completed:
Have you finished your work? Yes, *I've finished* it now.

PLUPERFECT

An action taking place before another action in the past:
The prices *had gone* up before we placed the order. I *had not noticed* this at the time.

Conditional past:
If we *had known* that prices were higher, we should have ordered the watches sooner.

Indirect speech:
He said that business *had been* fairly bad, but that he *had made* a small profit.

> *Perfect* is often used with: already, just, several times, since, for, not yet, ever, now, how long, so far, lately

PERFECT CONTINUOUS

Used as above with certain verbs when an action lasts for some time:
We *have been manufacturing* ski boots for forty years.

PERFECT GERUND

(rules as for Gerund and above).
We cannot place an order without *having seen* some samples. After *having checked* these, we shall let you know.

Exercises

1 Correct these sentences

1. We received the goods which you have delivered yesterday.
2. We have written last week stating that the prices were not suitable.
3. He asked me why I have not visited him before.
4. We gave our best attention to your inquiry.
5. How long do you learn English? I am learning since two years.
6. Have you telephoned Mr. Foster last Monday?
7. We cannot send a quotation without that we have listed the right prices.

2 Translate these sentences

1. Wann haben Sie die Zahlungen geleistet? Ich habe das Konto am Ende des letzten Monats beglichen.
2. Sie sind seit zehn Jahren unsere regelmässigen Kunden.
3. Da wir mit Ihnen noch nicht in Geschäftsbeziehungen stehen, benötigen wir zwei Referenzen.
4. Da diese Anfragen zufriedenstellend beantwortet worden sind, haben wir ein Kreditkonto für zukünftige Geschäftsabwicklungen eröffnet.
5. Es freut uns, die Namen von zwei Firmen anzugeben, mit denen wir seit Jahren regelmässige Geschäftsverbindungen haben.
6. Er hat unsern Brief noch nicht beantwortet; wir haben dem Besitzer gestern wieder geschrieben.
7. Wir haben soeben unseren neuesten Katalog herausgebracht.
8. Wann haben Sie Herrn Rainer zuletzt getroffen? Ich habe ihn seit vier oder fünf Wochen nicht gesehen.

9. Die Rechnungen wurden oft zu spät bezahlt, zum Teil erst nach Zahlungsaufforderungen.
10. Letzte Woche habe ich die in Ihrem Brief vom 9. März gewünschten Auskünfte erhalten.
11. Wie lange bist du schon [ein] Vertreter dieser Firma? Ich bin vor vier Jahren angestellt worden.
12. Hat Herr Taylor der Versicherungsgesellschaft den Betrag schon mitgeteilt?
13. Wo haben Sie den Brief der Firma Carlton & Co. hingelegt?
14. Die Ersatzteile wurden verschickt, bevor wir sie geprüft hatten.
15. Auf Ihre Anfrage haben wir am 20. Mai ein ausführliches Angebot unterbreitet.
16. Wir danken für Ihren Brief vom 2. dieses Monats und teilen Ihnen mit, dass die betreffende Ware gestern verschifft worden ist.
17. Unsere Speditionsabteilung hätte die bestellten Stoffe früher versandt, wenn es möglich gewesen wäre.
18. Die Ware ist noch nicht angekommen.

H. Some prepositions in use (I)

AT

at 11 o'clock	*um 11 Uhr*
at a fixed time/date	*zu einem bestimmten Zeitpunkt/Datum*
at the time of delivery	*zur Zeit der Lieferung*
at your earliest convenience	*sobald als möglich/sobald es Ihnen passt*
at once	*sofort*
at present	*gegenwärtig*
at the moment	*im Augenblick*
at a price of	*zu einem Preis von*
at 65 p per dozen/at 65 p a dozen	*zu 65 Pence das Dutzend*
at cost	*zum Selbstkostenpreis*
at an extra charge	*mit Zuschlag*
at a rate of interest	*zu einem Zinssatz*
to be at the office	*im Büro sein*
at the store	*im Warenhaus*
to look at	*anschauen*
to arrive at	*ankommen in*
to call at	*vorbeigehen*
to be at a person's disposal	*jemandem zur Verfügung stehen*
at least	*wenigstens/mindestens*
at all/not at all	*überhaupt/gar nicht*
at the suggestion of	*auf Anregung von*
at the request of/at your request	*auf Wunsch von/auf Ihren Wunsch, Antrag*

BY

by 15 September at the latest	bis spätestens am 15. September
by a certain date	bis zu einem bestimmten Datum

by water	auf dem Wasserweg
by train/by rail	mit der Bahn
by goods train	als Frachtgut
by fast train	als Eilgut
by air/by air freight	mit dem Flugzeug/als Luftfracht
by air mail	als Luftpost
by separate mail	mit besonderer/separater Post
by return of post	postwendend/umgehend
by express	als Eilsendung/Eilbrief
by mistake	irrtümlicherweise

to pay by instalments	in Raten bezahlen
to reduce by	ermässigen um
to profit by	Gewinn/Vorteil ziehen aus
Passive ... by	durch/von

FOR

your cheque for $ 20	Ihr Scheck von $ 20
an invoice for	eine Faktura von
an order for goods	eine Bestellung von Waren
quotation for goods	Angebot/Offerte von Waren
to pay for something	etwas bezahlen
for cash	gegen Barzahlung
for prompt payment	bei pünktlicher Zahlung
a demand for	Nachfrage nach

to ask for	bitten um/verlangen
to wait for	warten auf
to apologize for	um Entschuldigung bitten
to apply for	sich bewerben um
ready for dispatch	versandbereit
claim for compensation	Schadenersatzforderung
for this reason	aus diesem Grund

famous for	berühmt wegen
to be in the market for	Bedarf haben für
to depart for	abreisen nach
to look for	suchen/Ausschau halten nach

for instance	zum Beispiel
for the first time	zum erstenmal
for the attention of	zuhanden von
it is possible for me	es ist mir möglich

FROM

to hear from someone	hören von jemandem
to buy from someone	kaufen bei jemandem
to order from someone	bestellen von jemandem
to deliver from stock	ab Lager liefern
to take from	wegnehmen von

to deduct from	abziehen von
to differ from	abweichen von/sich unterscheiden von
different from	anders als
to protect from	schützen vor
from abroad	aus dem Ausland
open from Wednesdays to Fridays	mittwochs bis freitags geöffnet

IN

in future/in advance	in Zukunft/im voraus
in time	rechtzeitig/zur rechten Zeit
in the meantime	inzwischen
in (the course of) the next few days	im Laufe der nächsten Tage
in the afternoon/in the evening	nachmittags/abends
in turn	der Reihe nach
in fact	in der Tat
in accordance with	gemäss
in view of	mit Rücksicht auf
in reply to your	in Beantwortung Ihrer/als Antwort auf
in your letter	mit Ihrem Schreiben
in order	in Ordnung
in order to	um zu/damit
in heavy demand	sehr gesucht
in case (of)	falls
in your interests	in Ihrem Interesse
in our favour	zu unseren Gunsten
in this way	auf diese Art
to be in debt	verschuldet sein
in spite of	trotz
to be interested in	Interesse haben an/sich interessieren für
to deal in	handeln mit (etwas)
to succeed in	gelingen
to be unsuccessful (in)	nicht erfolgreich sein
we have pleasure in sending you	es freut uns, Ihnen ... zuzustellen
to have difficulty/trouble in	Schwierigkeit(en) haben um
in settlement of your	in Begleichung Ihrer
in possession of	im Besitz von
to be in the market for	Bedarf haben an
to get in touch	sich in Verbindung setzen
to invest money in	Geld anlegen in
rise in price	Verteuerung
reduction in price	Preisermässigung
delay in payment	Zahlungsverzögerung
to be in excess of	übersteigen
in comparison with	beim Vergleich mit
to have in stock	auf Lager haben

Exercises

1 Complete these sentences

1 Many thanks ... your letter.
2 We are interested ... your products.

3 At present we cannot deliver the goods ordered ... stock.
4 You will be in possession ... the goods ... 12 April.
5 They wish to place an order ... a large quantity.
6 The goods you supplied were different ... the samples.
7 We thank you ... advance ... a prompt reply.
8 We shall send you the illustrations ... our earliest convenience.
9 This important parcel is going to be sent ... air mail.
10 ... this reason I shall not be able to come ... time.
11 ... order to give you an opportunity to discuss further details, we shall wait ... his next letter.
12 We have plenty ... spare parts ... stock.
13 I heard ... my agent that you had been away ... two weeks.
14 Our customers are ... the market ... sports shoes.

2 Translate

1. Dieser Betrag kann von unserer Faktura abgezogen werden.
2. Wir brauchen die Uhren für das Weihnachtsgeschäft [Handel]. Ist es Ihnen möglich, diese rechtzeitig zu liefern?
3. Ich werde Ihnen die Versandpapiere umgehend zukommen lassen.
4. Die Ersatzteile sind gegenwärtig nicht am Lager, aber wir werden sie im Laufe der nächsten Woche sicher erhalten.
5. Der Einkaufschef der Firma Ritetime Watches wird Ihnen eine grössere Bestellung von Armbanduhren aufgeben.
6. Auf Anregung von Herrn Müller werden wir einen kaufmännischen Lehrling suchen.
7. Können sie das Plastikmaterial ab Lager liefern?
8. Wir müssen bis spätestens nächsten Montag eine Zusammenkunft vereinbaren.
9. Wollen Sie uns die Muster als Eilbrief zurücksenden.
10. Der Chef wird bald wieder im Büro sein.
11. Dieser Liegestuhl ist für Ihren Zweck sehr geeignet.
12. Sie haben uns Ihre Rechnung von Fr. 950.– zugestellt, jene von Fr. 120.– haben wir dagegen noch nicht erhalten.
13. Mit Rücksicht auf die lange Lieferfrist empfehlen wir Ihnen, die Büromöbel so bald als möglich zu bestellen.
14. Die Bank hat uns gemeldet, dass sie unsern Scheck von Fr. 2000.– Ihrem Konto gutgeschrieben hat.
15. Auf Wunsch unseres Vertreters werden wir die Preise um 3 % herabsetzen.

I. Some prepositions in use (II)

OF

date of delivery	*Lieferdatum*
date of your letter	*Datum Ihres Briefes*
your letter of yesterday's date	*Ihr gestriges Schreiben*

in the course of	*im Laufe von*
of late	*in letzter Zeit*
a cup of tea	*eine Tasse Tee*
a glass of beer	*ein Glas Bier*
a box of	*eine Schachtel ...*
a sample of	*ein Muster ...*
a copy of	*eine Kopie ...*
plenty of	*reichlich*
at the price of	*zum Preise von*
the amount of	*der Betrag von*
in settlement of	*in Begleichung*
conditions of sale	*Verkaufsbedingungen*
terms of payment	*Zahlungsbedingungen*
details of	*Einzelheiten*
cost of living	*Lebenshaltungskosten*
in receipt of your	*im Besitz Ihrer*
in possession of your	
in charge of	*beauftragt mit*
shortage of	*Knappheit an*
to consist of	*bestehen aus*
to remind of	*erinnern an*
made of	*aus ... gemacht*
balance of trade	*Handelsbilanz*

ON

on 11 April	*am 11. April*
on time	*pünktlich*
on arrival	*bei (der) Ankunft*
on receipt of	*beim Empfang*
on unpacking the goods	*beim Auspacken der Ware*
on checking the list	*bei der Kontrolle der Liste*
on comparing with	*beim Vergleich mit*
on the usual terms	*zu den gewohnten Bedingungen*
on certain/special terms	*zu gewissen/besonderen Bedingungen*
on condition that	*vorausgesetzt, dass*
on approval	*zur Ansicht*
cash on delivery	*Zahlung gegen Nachnahme*
a discount of 3% on prices quoted	*ein Skonto von 3% auf die angegebenen Preise*
on board	*an Bord*
free on board	*franko Schiff*
on request	*auf Verlangen/Wunsch*
on loan/on trial	*leihweise/probeweise*
(part) payment on account	*Anzahlung*
on purpose	*absichtlich*
to call on	*besuchen/vorbeikommen*
to depend on/upon	*abhängen von/sich verlassen auf*
to rely on someone	*sich auf jemanden verlassen*
to insist on	*beharren/bestehen auf*
on the phone	*am Telefon*
to draw on	*(Wechsel) ziehen auf*
a cheque on London	*Scheck auf London*

to spend money on	Geld aufwenden für
to receive information on	Auskunft erhalten über
on our part	unsere(rseits)
an expert on	Sachverständiger für
on the market	auf dem Markt
on hand	vorrätig

TO

in reply to	in Beantwortung/als Antwort auf
with reference to	in bezug/mit Bezug auf
with regard to	
referring to	bezugnehmend
according to	gemäss, laut
owing to	infolge
due to	zurückzuführen auf/infolge
subject to	unter der Bedingung/unterliegen
as to	hinsichtlich
to the value of	im Wert von
up to	bis (zu)
to be up to standard	Anforderungen genügen
to look forward to	sich freuen auf
to amount to	sich belaufen auf, betragen
to reduce to	ermässigen auf
to the credit	zugunsten
to the debit	zu Lasten
to apply to	sich melden/sich bewerben/anfragen
to complain to	sich beschweren/beklagen bei
to draw your attention to	Sie auf etwas aufmerksam machen
to agree to	zustimmen
to be obliged to someone	jemandem dankbar sein
we request you to (inf.)	wir bitten Sie
we advise you to (inf.)	wir raten Ihnen
in order to (inf.)	um zu ...

WITH

in accordance with	gemäss
with reference/regard to	mit Bezug auf
with many thanks	mit bestem Dank
with kind regards	mit freundlichen Grüssen
with great regret	mit grossem Bedauern
with the exception of	mit Ausnahme von/ausgenommen
an account with	ein Konto haben bei
together with	zusammen/samt
to enclose with	beilegen
to meet (with Am)	Zusammentreffen/kommen
to supply with	beliefern mit
to agree with	übereinstimmen/einverstanden sein mit
to tally with	übereinstimmen
to comply with a request	einem Wunsch entsprechen
to place an order with	Bestellung aufgeben bei
to deal with	behandeln/Handel treiben mit

to entrust us with your business	*uns Ihre Geschäfte anvertrauen*
to favour us with an order	*erteilen Sie uns bitte eine Bestellung*
to compare with	*vergleichen mit*
in comparison with	*beim Vergleich mit*
we are satisfied with	*wir sind zufrieden mit*

Exercises

1 Complete these sentences

1 Our traveller will call ... you next week.
2 ... reply ... your inquiry, we shall send you the book ... approval.
3 Please send us a sample ... your best quality coffee.
4 Can you supply us ... six dozen pairs?
5 We shall carry ... your order ... accordance .. your instructions.
6 This is ... reference ... your invoice ... yesterday's date.
7 May we remind you ... our cheque ... the credit ... Mr. Sims.
8 They compared the balance ... trade ... that of last year.
9 The prices are subject ... change without notice.
10 Would you let us have the information ... return ... mail.
11 I insist ... having an immediate reply ... my last letter.
12 Our forwarding agents will deal ... this consignment.

2 Translate

1. Wir können Ihre Bestellung unter folgenden Bedingungen annehmen.
2. Innert zwei Wochen wird Ihnen ein grösserer Auftrag erteilt.
3. Wir legen unserem Brief eine Kopie der Versandanzeige bei.
4. Diese Bestandteile könnten (vielleicht) in der Schublade aufbewahrt werden.
5. Das bestätigte Lieferdatum stimmt nicht mit unserer Bestellung überein.
6. Da unsere Vorräte zu Ende gehen, können wir Ihnen nur die Hälfte der bestellten Artikel zukommen lassen.
7. Wir hoffen, dass Sie uns bis am 10. August die Anzahlung machen werden.
8. Wir bestätigen den Empfang Ihres gestrigen Briefes.
9. Gemäss Ihren Angaben hätten wir mit den Schreibmaschinen (auch) die Ersatzteile erhalten sollen.
10. Zahlung: innert 30 Tagen abzüglich 2% Skonto oder 60 Tage netto.
11. Mit grossem Bedauern müssen wir Ihnen mitteilen, dass wir die versandten Trommeln noch nicht erhalten haben.
12. Wir beharren darauf [your sending], dass Sie die Uhren sofort als Luftpost schicken.
13. Unser Vertreter wird am Freitag bei Ihnen vorbeikommen, um Ihnen unsere Auswahlsendung zu zeigen.
14. Da die Firma uns nicht bekannt ist, raten wir Ihnen, Erkundigungen einzuziehen.

Appendix I

Abbreviations and Signs

A Selection for general and commercial use

@	at	*zu*
a/c	account, account current	*Konto, Rechnung, Kontokorrent*
a/d	after date	*nach Datum*
* A.D.	*Anno Domini*	*im Jahre des Herrn*
* ad advt.	advertisement	*Inserat, Anzeige*
a.m.	*ante meridiem,* before noon	*vormittags*
approx.	approximate(ly)	*ungefähr*
A/S	account sales	*Verkaufsabrechnung*
* Asst.	Assistant	*Assistent*
* B.A.	Bachelor of Arts	*Bakkalaureus der humanistischen Fakultät*
* B.C.	Before Christ	*vor Christus*
B/D	Bank(ers) draft	*Banküberweisung*
B/E	Bill of Exchange	*Wechsel, Tratte*
B of E	Bank of England	*Englische Nationalbank*
b/f	brought forward	*Übertrag*
B/L	Bill of Lading	*Konossoment*
BR	British Railways	*Britische Eisenbahnen*
* Bros.	brothers	*Gebrüder*
B/S	bill of sale	*Liefer-, Verpfändungsschein*
* B.Sc.	Bachelor of Science	*Bakkalaureus der naturwissenschaftlichen Fakultät*
C	Centigrade	*Celsius*
* c.	cent(s)	*Cent*
cc	carbon copy	*Durchschlag*
cv. *confer*	compare	*vergleiche*
c/f	carried forward	*übertragen*
C & F	cost and freight	*Kosten und Fracht*
CIF	cost, insurance, freight	*Kosten, Versicherung und Fracht*
* cm.	centimetre(s)	*Zentimeter*
* Co.	company	*Gesellschaft*
* contd.	continued	*fortgesetzt*
c/o	care of	*per Adresse*
COD	cash on delivery	*per Nachnahme*
C/N	credit note	*Gutschrift*
* cr.	credit, creditor	*Kredit, Gläubiger*
* cwt.	hundredweight(s)	*Zentner*
D/A	documents against acceptance	*(Versand) Papiere gegen Akzept*
d/d	days after date, dated	*Tage nach Datum, datiert*
*dbt.	debit	*Debit*
*dept.	department	*Abteilung*
div.	dividend	*Dividende*
DM		*Deutsche Mark*
D/N	debit note	*Lastschrift*

$ dol.	dollar(s)	*Dollar*
D/P	documents against payment	*(Versand) Papiere gegen Zahlung*
* Dr.	doctor, debtor	*Doktor, Schuldner*
d/s	days after sight	*Tage nach Sicht*
E	East	*Ost*
E.E.	errors excepted	*Irrtum vorbehalten*
E. & O.E.	errors and omissions excepted	*Irrtümer und Auslassungen vorbehalten*
EC	European Community	*EG*
* e.g.	*(exempli gratia)* for example	*zum Beispiel*
* enc. encl.	enclosure	*Beilage*
* Esq.	Esquire	*Höflichkeitsform eines Herrn*
* etc.	et cetera	*usw.*
* exp.	expense(s)	*(Un)Kosten*
F.	Fahrenheit, franc	*Grad Temperatur*
FAS	free alongside ship	*frei Schiffsseite*
FOB	free on board	*frei an Bord*
FOR	free on rail	*frei Versandbahnhof*
* fr.	franc(s)	*Frank(en)*
* ft.	foot, feet	*Fuss (30 cm)*
* fwd.	forward	*vom Empfänger zu bezahlen*
GB	Great Britain	*Grossbritannien*
GPO	General Post Office	*Britisches Postamt*
HMC	His (Her) Majesty's Customs	*Britisches Zollamt*
HMS	His (Her) Majesty's Ship	*Britisches Schiff*
* h.p.	hire purchase, horse power	*Ratenzahlung, Pferdestärke*
* i.e.	*(id est)* that is	*das heisst*
Inc.	Incorporated	*Aktiengesellschaft (U.S.)*
* in.	inch(es)	*Zoll (2,54 cm)*
* inst.	instant	*dieses Monats*
* inv.	invoice	*Faktur*
IOU	I owe you	*Schuldschein*
* jr. jun.	junior	*junior*
* kg.	kilogramme(s)	*Kilogramm*
* km.	kilometre(s)	*Kilometer*
£	*(Libra, e)* pound(s) sterling	*Pfund (sterling)*
lab	laboratory	*Laboratorium*
* lb.	*(Libra, e)* pound(s) weight	*Pfund (454 Gramm)*
L/C	letter of credit	*Akkreditiv, Kreditbrief*
* Ltd.	Limited	*Aktiengesellschaft* (Br.)

* m.	meter, million	*Meter, Million*
* M.A.	Master of Arts	*Magister der philosophischen Fakultät*
* M.D.	Doctor of Medicine	*Doktor der Medizin*
* Messrs.	Messieurs	*Herren*
* mm.	millimetre(s)	*Millimeter*
MP	Member of Parliament	*Parlamentsmitglied*
* mo. mos	month, months	*Monat(e)*
MO	money order	*Geldüberweisung*
* MS. MSS.	manuscript, manuscripts	*Manuskript(e)*
MS	motor ship	*Motorschiff*
Mr.	Mister (not to be written out)	*Herr*
* Mrs.	Missus (not to be written out)	*Frau*
MV	motor vessel	*Motorschiff*

N	North	*Norden*
* nr.	near	*bei*
* n.b.	*(nota bene)* note well	*zur Beachtung*
* No. Nos.	number(s)	*Nummer(n)*
NW	North-West	*Nordwest*

o/a	on account	*als Anzahlung*
o/d	on demand	*auf Verlangen, auf Sicht*
OD	overdraft	*Überziehung (eines Bankkontos)*
* O.K.	all correct	*in Ordnung*
* oz.	ounce(s)	*Unze (28,3 Gramm)*

p	penny, pence	
* p.a.	per annum	*jährlich*
* p.pp.	page, pages	*Seite(n)*
* p.c. %	postcard, per cent	*Briefkarte, Prozent*
* pd.	paid	*bezahlt*
per pro	p.p. *per procura*	*per Prokura*
* p.m.	*(post meridiem)* after noon	*nachmittags*
PO	Post Office	*Postamt*
* P.S.	postscript	*Nachschrift*
* P.T.O.	please turn over	*bitte wenden*

* rcd.	received	*erhalten*
* R.S.V.P.	*répondez s'il vous plait*	*um Antwort wird gebeten*
* ref. re	(with) reference (to)	*betrifft*
* regd.	registered	*eingeschrieben*
* Rly.	Railway	*Eisenbahn*
r. pd.	reply paid	*Rückantwort bezahlt*

S/A	statement of account	*Kontoauszug*
* S.A.E.	stamped addressed envelope	*frankiertes Antwortkuvert*
SE	South-East	*Süd-Ost*
S	South	*Süd*
* Sec.	Secretary	*Sekretär(in)*
* Sig.	signature, signed	*Unterschrift, unterschrieben*

S/N	shipping note	*Schiffszettel*
* sq.	square	*Quadrat-*
SS	steamship	*Dampfer*
Sfr. Sw.fr.	Swiss Francs	*Schweizerfranken*
* t.	ton(s)	*Tonne(n)*
* tr.	translate, -tion	*übersetzen, Übersetzung*
UK	United Kingdom	*Vereinigtes Königreich*
* U.N.	United Nations	*Vereinte Nationen*
* U.S.A.	United States of America	*Vereinigte Staaten von Nordamerika*
* U.S.S.R.	Union of Soviet Socialist Republics	*Union der Sozialistischen Sowjetrepubliken*
* var.	various	*verschiedene*
via	by way of	*über*
* viz.	*(videlicet)* namely	*nämlich, das heisst*
* vol.	volume	*Rauminhalt, Band*
W	west	*Westen*
w.a.m.	words a minute	*Wörter pro Minute*
w.p.m.	words per minute	
* wt.	weight	*Gewicht*
* yd.	yard(s)	*91,44 cm*
* yr.	year(s), your	*Jahr(e)*

* *The Oxford English Dictionary gives these abbreviations without a full stop. In Webster's American Dictionary and in American usage the stop is generally shown. Whichever form is chosen, uniformity should be maintained throughout a letter or report.*

Word Lists

ability, Fähigheit
access, Zugriff
acceptance, Annahme
accommodation, Unterkunft
accompany, to, begleiten
accordingly, entsprechend
account, Rechnung, Konto
on no account, unter keinen Umständen
account sales, Verkaufsabrechnung
accountancy, Rechnungswesen, Buchführung
accounting, Buchhaltung
accuracy, Genauigkeit, Sorgfalt
accustom (to), to, gewöhnen (an)
achieve, to, erreichen
acknowledge, to, zugeben, bestätigen
acknowledg(e)ment, Bestätigung
acquaintance, Bekanntschaft, Bekannte(r)
acquire, to, anschaffen
act, to, auftreten
actual, eigentlich
actually, tatsächlich
ad, Inserat
adapt, to, anpassen
add, to, beifügen
addition, Zusatz
additional, zusätzlich
adequate, angemessen, genügend
adjust, to, anpassen
adjustment, Einstellung, Regulierung
admit, to, zugeben
adopt, to, übernehmen
advantage, Vorteil
advantageous, vorteilhaft
adverse, ungünstig
advertise, to, inserieren
advertiser, Inserent
advertising, Werbung
advertisement, Inserat
advice note, Versandanzeige
affect, to, beeinflussen
afford, to, sich leisten
agency, Agentur, Vertretung
aggressive, agressiv, angriffig
agreement, Übereinkunft
air waybill, Luftfrachtbrief
aircraft, Flugzeug
alteration, Änderung
alternative, alternativ
annual, jährlich

apologize, to, entschuldigen
appearance, Aussehen
applicable, anwendbar
applicant, Bewerber
application, Bewerbung
apply, to, ersuchen, bewerben, beantragen, sich wenden
appointment, Verabredung
approach, to, sich nähern, angehen
appropriate, angemessen, geeignet
approve, to, zustimmen
approximately, ungefähr
area, Gebiet
arrange, to, (an)ordnen, absprechen
arrangement, Abmachung, Vorbereitung
arrears, Rückstände, Schulden
artifical silk, Kunstseide
assets, Aktiva
assistance, Hilfe, Beistand
association, Verbindung
assume, to, annehmen
assurance, Ver-, Zusicherung
astonishing, erstaunlich
at home and abroad, im In- und Ausland
attach, to, beifügen, beiheften
attend, to, teilnehmen, beiwohnen
automate, to, automatisieren
automation, Automatisierung
availability, Verfügbarkeit
aviation, Luftfahrt
backing, Rückhalt, Unterstützung
balance, Saldo
bale, Ballen
banker, Bankier
barrel, Fass
barter, to, austauschen
base, to, basieren
be at fault, to, schuld sein
be convenient, to, gelegen sein
be due, to, fällig sein
be in excess of, to, überschreiten
be in existence, to, bestehen
bearer cheque, Inhabercheck
beforehand, vorgängig, zuvor
behaviour, Verhalten, Betragen
beneficiary, Begünstigter
benefit, Vorteil, Nutzen
bi-lingual, Zweisprachig
bill of lading, Frachtbrief, Konnossement
bond, Obligation
branch, Filiale

branch office, Zweigniederlassung
brand, Marke, Sorte
brisk, lebhaft
broker, Makler
bulk cargo, Massengüter
burglary, Einbruch
business relationship, Geschäftsbeziehung
by means of, mit Hilfe von, (ver)mittels
by return (of) mail, postwendend
calculating machine, Rechenmaschine
campaign, Kampagne
cancel, to, annullieren
capital appreciation, Kapitalzuwachs
cardboard, Pappe, Kartonpapier
career, Laufbahn
cargo, Ladung
carriage, Transport(kosten), Fracht(gebühr)
carriage forward, unfranko
carriage paid, franko
carrier, Transportunternehmer, Frachtführer
carry out, to, ausführen, betreiben
carton, Pappschachtel
case, Fall, Kiste
cash dispenser, Bargeldautomat
cash on delivery (COD), bar bei Lieferung, gegen Nachnahme
cash receipt, Quittung
cash with order (CWO), Vorausbezahlung, bar bei Bestellung
cash, to, einlösen
cattle, Vieh
cause, to, verursachen
caution, Vorsicht
cautious, vorsichtig
centre, to, zentrieren
certificate, Zeugnis
certificate of origin, Ursprungsbescheinigung, Ursprungszeugnis
cfm (= confirm), bestätigen
chairman, Vorsitzender
chamber of commerce, Handelskammer
character, Zeichen
charges, (Un)Kosten
checking account (US), Kontokorrent
cheque with restrictive endorsement, gekreuzter Check, Verrechnungscheck
cif/cost, insurance, freight, Kosten, Versicherung und (See-)Fracht
circulation, Auflage
claim for compensation, Ersatzforderung

collection, Inkasso, Einziehung
collection agency, Inkassobüro
collection letter, Mahnbrief
column, Kolonne
come to terms, to, sich einig werden
command, Beherrschung
commencement, Beginn
commerce, Handelsverkehr
commercial, Werbesendung, Werbespot
commitment, Verpflichtung
company, Gesellschaft
compare favourably with, günstig abschneiden im Vergleich mit
compel, to, zwingen, nötigen
compensate, to, entschädigen
compensation, Entschädigung
competitive, Konkurrenzfähig
competitor, Konkurrent
compile, to, zusammenstellen
complaint, Beschwerde, Mängelrüge
complex, vielfältig, komplex
complicated, kompliziert
compose, to, zusammensetzen, aufsetzen
comprise, to, umfassen
compulsory, obligatorisch
computing science, Computerkunde, Informatik
concerning, betreffend
confident, zuversichtlich
confidential, vertraulich
confirm, to, bestätigen
confirmation, Bestätigung
confuse, to, verwirren, verwechseln
connection, Verbindung
consider, to, in Betracht ziehen
considerable, erheblich, bedeutend
consideration, Erwägung, Überlegung
consignment, Versand
consignor, Absender
contain, to, beinhalten
contents, Inhalt
contest, Wettbewerb
contribute, to, beitragen
convey, to, übermitteln, befördern
cordial, herzlich
couch, to, in Worte fassen
counter-offer, Gegenofferte
counter-proposal, Gegenvorschlag
countless, zahllos
course, Kurs, Lehrgang
cover, to, umfassen
covering letter, Begleitbrief
crate, Harass, Lattenkiste
crated, in Harasse verpackt

201

create, to, (er)schaffen, erzeugen
credit rating, Kreditwürdigkeit
creditor, Gläubiger
cross-checking, kontrollieren und gegenkontrollieren
crossed cheque, gekreuzter Check, Verrechnungscheck
crude, roh, hier: Rohöl
currency, Währung
current account, Kontokorrent
currently, zur Zeit
curriculum vitae, Lebenslauf
customs, Zoll
customs clearance, Zollabfertigung
daisy wheel, Druckrad
damage, Schaden
damage, to, beschädigen
data protection, Datenschutz
data sheet, Lebenslauf
date, to, datieren
deal with, to, behandeln, erledigen, regeln
debtor, Schuldner
debugging, Fehlersuche
decade, Jahrzehnt
deck chair, Liegestuhl
declaration, (Zoll)Erklärung
decline, to, abnehmen
decrease, to, abnehmen, sinken
delay, to, aufschieben, verzögern
delegate, to, delegieren
deliver, to, liefern
delivery, Lieferung
delivery note, Lieferschein
demand, Nachfrage
dent, to, einbeulen, eindrücken
deposit account, Depositenkonto
design, Formgebung, Konstruktion
design, to, entwerfen, entwickeln
destination, Bestimmung(sort), Ziel
detail, to, genau schildern, einzeln aufzählen
devote, to, widmen
diary, Tagebuch, Taschenkalender
differ, to, abweichen
dimension, Abmessung, Mass
disappoint, to, enttäuschen
discharge, to, entladen
discount, Rabatt
discrepancy, Unstimmigkeit
disk, Scheibe (hier: Plattenspeicher)
display, Auslage
display screen, Bildschirm
dispose of, to, veräussern

distributor, Verteiler, Wiederverkäufer
divide, to, trennen
docks, Hafen(anlagen)
(documentary) letter of credit, Akkreditiv
domain, Gebiet, Domäne
draft, Entwurf
draft, to, entwerfen
drawer, Schublade
drum, Trommel
due, fällig
due date, Verfalldatum
due to, wegen, verursacht durch
dull, eintönig
duplicate, to, vervielfältigen
durable, dauerhaft, robust
economic, wirtschafts-
economical, ökonomisch, wirtschaftlich
education, Ausbildung, Erziehung
effect, Auswirkung
effect, to, ausführen
eliminate, to, eliminieren, vernichten
elsewhere, anderswo
employ, to, einstellen, einsetzen, gebrauchen
employee, Angestellter
employer, Arbeitgeber
employment, Stellung, Beschäftigung
enable, to, ermöglichen
enclose, to, beilegen
enclosure, Beilage
encounter, to, begegnen
encourage, to, ermutigen
endeavour, Bemühung
endorse, to, indossieren
ensure, to, sicherstellen, gewährleisten
entail, to, beinhalten
enter, to, buchen
entrust with, to, betrauen mit
entry, Einsendung, Eingang
environment, Umgebung
equipment, Ausstattung, Anlage, Apparatur, Ausrüstung
essential, wesentlich
establish, to, gründen
estate agent, Grundstückmakler
estimate, Schätzung, Voranschlag
estimate, to, schätzen
evidently, offenbar, offentsichtlich
examine, to, (über)prüfen
exceed, to, übersteigen, übertreffen
exclude, to, ausschliessen
execute an order, to, eine Bestellung ausführen

execution (of an order), Ausführung
exhibition, Ausstellung
expand, to, ausbreiten
expense, Ausgabe
expensive, teuer
experience, Erfahrung
expire, to, verfallen, ablaufen
express, to, ausdrücken
extend, to ausweiten
extension, Verlängerung, Erweiterung, Ausbau
extensive, ausgedehnt
extensively, weitgehend
extent, Umfang
extremely, ausserordentlich
facilitate, to, erleichtern
facility, Möglichkeit, Erleichterung
fail, to, unterlassen, versäumen
fair, Messe
familiar, vertraut
fault-finding, Fehlersuche
faulty, mangelhaft
favourable, günstig, vorteilhaft
feature, Merkmal, (Gesichts)Punkt, Spezialartikel, Rubrik
fee, Honorar
feed, to, füttern, eingeben (Daten)
figure, Zahl
file a claim, to, Forderung einreichen, Schaden melden
file maintenance procedure, Dateiwartung
final, definitiv
financial statement, Erfolgsrechnung
firm, Firma, Unternehmen, fest
firm offer, verbindl. Angebot
fixed, fest stehend, fixiert
flexible, flexibel, beweglich
flourish, to, blühen
fluctuation, Schwankung
fob/free on board, franko Schiff
footwear, Schuhwerk
for instance, zum Beispiel
form, Formular
fortnightly, vierzehntäglich
forwarding agent, Spediteur
fragile, zerbrechlich
freight, Fracht
frequently, häufig
fuel, Treibstoff
furnish with, to, ausstatten mit
gap, Lücke
get low, to, Tiefstand erreichen
go astray, to, in die Irre gehen, abhanden kommen
gold bar, Goldbarren
goods, Güter, Ware
grade, Qualität
grant, to, gewahren, einräumen
grateful, dankbar
handle, to, handhaben, hantieren, abwickeln
handsome, hübsch, stattlich
hardly, kaum
heading, Überschrift
honour, Ehre
huge, enorm
i.e., d.h. (das heisst)
ignore, to, ignorieren, nicht beachten
import duties, Importabgaben
improve, to, verbessern
in addition, darüber hinaus, zusätzlich
inadequate, unzulänglich
in advance, im voraus
in confidence, vertraulich
in due course, zur gegebenen Zeit
in duplicate, im Doppel
in heavy demand, stark gefragt
in our favour, zu unseren Gunsten
in question, in Frage stehend
in short supply, knapp
in the form of, in Form von
in transit, unterwegs, auf dem Transport
include, to, enthalten
included, inbegriffen
inconvenience, Unannehmlichkeit
inconvenient, lästig, ungelegen
incorporate, to, aufnehmen, miteinschliessen
incur, to, erleiden, auf sich laden
indent, Warenbezug
independent, selbständig
index, Index, Register
indicate, to, angeben, anzeigen
inferior, minderwertig
influence, to, beeinflussen
inform, to, mitteilen, informieren
infrequently, unregelmässig, hie und da
inheritance, Erbschaft
initial, erste
inland, inländisch
inquirer, Anfragender, Fragesteller
inquiry agency, Auskunftei
inquiry/enquiry, Anfrage
insert, to, einsetzen
insist on, to, bestehen auf
inspection, Überprüfung
instance, Beispiel, Fall

instantly, sofort
insurance, Versicherung
insure, to, versichern
insurer, Versicherer
interest, Zins
interpret, to, auslegen
intrigued, gefesselt, erstaunt
inventory, Inventar, Lagerbestand
investigate, to, untersuchen
investment, Investition, Anlage
investment counselling, Anlageberatung
invite, to, einladen
invoice, Rechnung
involve, to, beteiligen, einschliessen
irrevocable, unwiderruflich
issue, to, (her)ausgeben
item, Artikel
itinerary, Reiseplan
job card, Arbeitskarte
justify, to, rechtfertigen
keyboard, Tastatur
kind regards, beste Grüsse
knowledge, Kenntnis
lack, Fehlen, Mangel
lately, neuerdings
launch, to, lancieren
lawsuit, Prozess
leading, führend
leaflet, Flugblatt, Prospekt
legally binding, rechtlich bindend
letter of credit, Akkreditiv
liability, Haftung
libel, Verleumdung
lid, Deckel
lighter, Feuerzeug
limit, to, begrenzen
limited, beschränkt, begrenzt
lining, Auskleidung, Futter
liquid, flüssig
list, to, auflisten
literally, buchstäblich
load, to, (auf)laden
loan, Kredit
locally, örtlich
loss, Verlust, Schaden
lump sum, Pauschalabfindung
mail, Post, Versand
mailing list, Versandliste, Adressliste
maintain, to, (aufrecht)erhalten
management, Direktion
manual, manuell, Anleitung
manufacture, to, herstellen
manufactured goods, Fertigprodukte
manufacturer, Hersteller
marine insurance, Transportversicherung
meantime, Zwischenzeit
media mix, Kombination des Medieneinsatzes
medium, Vermittlung, vermittels
meet one's liabilities, seinen Verpflichtungen nachkommen, begleichen
meet the requirements, Anforderungen entsprechen
meeting, Treffen, Sitzung
memory, Gedächtnis, (Computer) Speicher
merchandise, Ware
merchant, Kaufmann, Handelsherr
message, Mitteilung, Botschaft
message slip, Mitteilungszettel, Memo
minor, geringfügig
minutes, Notizen, Protokoll
misuse, Missbrauch
money-lender, Geldverleiher
motor accident, Verkehrsunfall
mutual, gegenseitig
neat, ordentlich, übersichtlich
need, Bedürfnis
negligence, Nachlässigkeit
negotiable, verkehrsfähig
non-stick coating, nichthaftender Belag
not ... either, auch nicht
note, to, Kenntnis nehmen von
notice, Mitteilung, Meldung, (An)kündigung
notification, Benachrichtigung, Anzeige
notify, to, mitteilen, anzeigen
numerous, zahlreich
obligation, Verpflichtung
oblige, to, nötigen, zwingen
observe, to, beachten
obtain, to, erlangen, erhalten
obtainable, erhältlich
obviously, offensichtlich
occasionally, gelegentlich
of consideration, von Belang
offer, to, anbieten
omission, Unterlassung, Versäumnis
on a cash basis, gegen bar
on deposit, in der Einlage
on his/her own account, auf eigene Rechnung
on our behalf, für uns, zu unseren Gunsten
on our part, unsererseits
on-line, direkte Verbindung mit/zu

operation, Bedienung
operator, Bedienungsperson
opportune, vorteilhaft
optical reader, optischer Lesestift/ Belegleser
order, Bestellung
order form, Bestellformular
outline, Umriss
outstanding, ausstehend
over and over again, wieder und immer wieder
overdraft, Überziehung
overdue, überfällig
overlook, to, übersehen
oversight, Versehen
overturn, to, umkippen
owe, to, schulden
package, Verpackung, Paket
packing, Verpackung
paragraph, Abschnitt, Absatz
paramount, ausschlaggebend, überragend
parcel, Paket
part, Teil
particular, bestimmte
particularly, besonders
particulars, Einzelheiten, Angaben
pass a resolution, to, Beschluss verabschieden
pattern, Muster, Vorlage
pave the way, to, den Weg bahnen
payee, Zahlungsempfänger
payment on account, Teilzahlung
per annum, pro Jahr
perfect, to, verbessern
perform, to, ausführen, verrichten
peripherals, periphere Einheit
perishables, leicht verderbliche Waren
personalise, to, personalisieren
physics, naturwissenschaftlich
policy, Police
policyholder, Versicherungsnehmer
position, Stelle
possession, Besitz
post, Stelle
postpone, to, aufschieben
prefer, to, vorziehen
preference, Vorliebe
premium, Prämie
present, anwesend
prevent, to, verhindern
previously, früher, vorher
print-out, Computerausdruck
printed, gedruckt

printed matter, Drucksache
printer, Drucker
proceeds, Erlös
process, to, ausführen, verarbeiten
profit, Gewinn
promote, to, fördern, unterstützen
promotion, Beförderung, Aufstieg
prompt, umgehend
proof, Beweis
proper, schicklich, anständig
property, Eigentum, Grundstück
proposal, Vorschlag
prospect, Aussicht
prospective, voraussichtlich, künftig
protect from, to, schützen vor
provide, to, beliefern, versehen, versorgen
provided, vorausgesetzt
provisional, provisorisch, vorläufig
publicity, Werbung
purchase, to, kaufen, anschaffen
purpose, Absicht, Zweck
qualification, Fähigkeit
quality, Beschaffenheit
quantity, Menge
quarter, Quartal
quarterly, vierteljährlich
query, Rückfrage
questionnaire(s), Umfrage, Fragebogen
quite some, ziemlich viel
quotation, Preisangabe, Notierung
quote, to, angeben, (Kurse) notieren
rack, Gestell
railway siding, Anschlussgleis
range, Sortiment
rate, Tarif
raw material, Rohmaterial
re-order, to, nachbestellen
reach an agreement, to, Übereinkunft erlangen
reasonable, vernünftig
recent, kürzlich
recipient, Empfänger
recommend, to, empfehlen
recommendation, Empfehlung
record, Unterlage, Aufzeichnung
record, to, aufzeichnen, erfassen
recover, to, wieder einbringen, einziehen
reduce, to, vermindern, reduzieren
refer to, to, sich beziehen auf
referee, Referent, Schiedsrichter
reference, Beleg, Bezugnahme
refuse, to, verweigern

regard, to, betrachten
regarding, betreffend
register (a letter), to, einschreiben
registered, eingeschrieben
regret, to, bedauern
regular, regelmässig
regular customer, Stammkunde
reinsurance, Rückversicherung
reject, to, ablehnen, zurückweisen
relevant, massgebend, wichtig, entsprechend, einschlägig
reliable, zuverlässig
reluctant, wiederstrebend
rely on, to, sich verlassen auf
remainder, Rest
reminder, Mahnung
rent, Miete
rental, Mietbetrag
reorder, to, nachbestellen
repayable, rückzahlbar
repayment, Rückzahlung
repeat order, Nachbestellung, neuerliche Bestellung
replacement, Ersatz
replenish, to, ergänzen, (wieder)auffüllen
report, Bericht
representative, Vertreter
reputable, angesehen
request, to, ersuchen
require, to, verlangen
requirements, Bedarf, Anforderungen
resale, Wiederverkauf
research, Forschung
reserve the right, to, Recht vorbehalten
residence, Aufenthalt, Wohnsitz
responsibility, Verantwortung
responsible, verantwortlich, zuverlässig
resumé, Zusammenfassung, Lebenslauf
resume, to, fortsetzen
retailer, Detaillist, Einzelhändler
retire, to, in Pension gehen
retooling, Umrüsten
retrieve, to, wiedergewinnen, abrufen
rise, to, steigen
salary, Gehalt, Salär
sample, Muster
save, to, sparen
savings, Spargeld, Ersparnis
savings account, Sparkonto, Sparguthaben
scientist, Wissenschafter
screen, (Bild)Schirm, Leinwand

secure, to, sichern, vertäuen
securities, Effekten, Wertschriften
security, Sicherheit
selection, Auswahl
semi-finished product, Halbfabrikat
sentence, Satz
separate, to, (ab)sondern, (aus)scheiden
set out, to, darlegen, festsetzen
setback, Rückschlag
settle a deal, to, Geschäft abschliessen
settle a debt, to, Schuld begleichen
share, Aktie, Anteil
sheet, Blatt
shelf, Fach, Regal
shipmaster, Kapitän
shipment, Lieferung
shipper, Spediteur, Verschiffer
short shipment, Manko
shortly, bald
sight draft, Sichtwechsel
sign, to, unterschreiben
signature, Unterschrift
similar, gleichartig, ähnlich
simplify, to, erleichtern, vereinfachen
sincere, aufrichtig
sincerely yours, Mit freundlichen Grüssen
size, Grösse
slack, flau, lustlos
slightly, ein wenig
sole, alleinig
solution, Lösung
solvency, Zahlungsfähigkeit
sort, to, sortieren
spare parts, Ersatzteile
specification, Spezifikation, Einzelvorschrift
speed, Schnelligkeit, Geschwindigkeit, Tempo
speedy, schnell, zügig
spot price, Marktpreis
spread, to, ausbreiten, verteilen
stack, to, stapeln
stainless, rostfrei
standardize, to, vereinheitlichen
standing, Ruf, Ansehen
state, to, feststellen
statement, Aussage
statement of account, Kontoauszug
status inquiry, Bonitätsauskunft, Erkundigung
stipulate, to, ausbedingen
stock, Lager

stock records, Lagerliste, Vorratsliste
stockkeeper, Magaziner, Lagerist
stocks, Aktien, Wertpapiere
storage, Lagerung
store, to, lagern
straightforward, einfach
stringent, streng
subject to, abhängig von, vorbehältlich
subject to confirmation, Bestätigung vorbehalten
subject to goods being unsold, Zwischenverkauf vorbehalten
submit, to, vorlegen, unterbreiten
subsidiary, Tochterunternehmen
suit, to, entsprechen, sich eignen
suitability, Eignung
suitable, passend
summary, Zusammenfassung
supervision, Aufsicht, Kontrolle
supervisor, Kontrolleur, Aufseher
supplement, to, ergänzen
supplier, Anbieter, Lieferant
supply, to, bereitstellen, beschaffen
survey, Gutachten, Umfrage
surveyor, Inspektor
table, Tabelle
tabulate, to, tabellarisch (an)ordnen
take advantage of, to, Gebrauch machen von
take legal action, to, Rechtsweg beschreiten
take notes, to, Notizen machen
take stock, to, Inventur machen
take up references, to, Referenzen ermitteln
tally to, übereinstimmen
tape, Band
task, Aufgabe
tax, Steuer
tend, to, tendieren, neigen
terms of payment, Zahlungsbedingungen
territory, Gebiet
testimonial, Zeugnis
theft, Diebstahl
third party liability, Haftpflicht
thoroughly, gründlich
threat, Gefahr, Drohung
time-consuming, zeitraubend
topic, Thema, Traktandum
trade, Handel
trade index, Branchenverzeichnis
trader, Händler
transaction, (Geschäfts)abschluss, geschäftliches Unternehmen
transfer, Überweisung
treat, to, behandeln
trial order, Probeauftrag
trust, Vertrauen
trustworthy, vertrauenswürdig
turnover, Umsatz
typical, typisch, bezeichnend
tyre, Pneu
unconditonally, bedingungslos
under separate cover, gesondert
underwriter, Versicherer
unemployment, Arbeitslosigkeit
unfailing, unfehlbar
unfavourable, ungünstig
unit, Einheit
universal, tool, Universalgerät
unload, to, entladen, löschen (Ladung)
unsatisfactory, unbefriedigend
upset, to, bestürzen, aus der Fassung bringen
vacancy, Vakanz, offene Stelle
valid, gültig
valuables, Wertsachen
van, Lastwagen, Lieferwagen
varied, vielfältig, mannigfältig
variety, Abwechslung
vast, riesig
verbal, mündlich
vicinity, Nähe, Nachbarschaft
video display unit, Bildschirm
view, Ansicht, Meinung
viewer, (Fernseh)zuschauer
war risk, Kriegsrisiko
warn of, to, warnen vor
warning note, Warnzeichen
waterproof (paper), wasserdicht
watertight (cases), wasserdicht
weigh, to, wägen
wholesaler, Grossist
wholesaling, Grosshandel
withdraw, to, abheben
word processing, Textverarbeitung
word processor, Schreibautomat
wrap, to, einwickeln
yield, Ertrag, Rendite

Wörterverzeichnis

abheben, withdraw, to
abhängig von, subject to
ablaufen, expire, to
ablehnen, reject, to
Abmachung, arrangement
Abmessung, dimension
abnehmen, decrease, to, decline, to
Abschnitt, paragraph
Absender, consignor
Absicht, purpose
absondern, separate, to
absprechen, arrange, to
Abwechslung, variety
abweichen, differ, to
abwickeln, handle, to
ähnlich, similar
Änderung, alteration
AG, Inc. (Incorporated) *Am.*, Ltd (Limited Company) *Brit.*
Agentur, agency
aggressiv, aggressive
Akkreditiv, (documentary) letter of credit
Aktien, shares, stocks
Aktiva, assets
alleinig, sole
alternativ, alternative
anbieten, offer, to
Anbieter, supplier
anderswo, elsewhere
Anforderungen entsprechen, meet the requirements
Anfrage, inquiry/enquiry
anfragender, inquirer
angeben, quote, to, indicate, to
Angelegenheit, matter
angemessen, appropriate, adequate
angesehen, reputable
Anlage, investment, equipment
Anlageberatung, investment counselling
Anleitung, manual
Annahme, acceptance
annehmen, assume, to
annullieren, cancel, to
anordnen, arrange, to
anpassen, adapt, to
anschaffen, acquire, to/purchase, to
Anschlussgleis, railway siding
Ansicht, view
Anteil, share
anwendbar, applicable

anwesend, present
Anzeige, notification
anzeigen, notify, to
Apparatur, equipment
Arbeitgeber, employer
Arbeitskarte, job card
Arbeitslosigkeit, unemployment
Artikel, item
auf eigene Rechnung, on his/her own account
Aufenthalt, residence
Aufgabe, task
aufladen, load, to
Auflage, circulation
auflisten, list, to
aufnehmen, incorporate, to
aufrechterhalten, maintain, to
aufrichtig, sincere
aufschieben, delay, to, postpone, to
Aufseher, supervisor
Aufsicht, supervision
auftreten, act, to
aufzeichnen, record, to
ausbedingen, stipulate, to
Ausbildung, education
ausbreiten, spread, to, expand, to
ausdrücken, express, to
ausführen, effect, to, perform, to, carry out, to, process, to
Ausführung, execution (of an order)
Ausgaben, expense
ausgeben *(i.S.v. veröffentlichen)*, issue, to
ausgedehnt, extensive
Auskleidung, lining
Auskunftei, inquiry agency
Auslage, display
auslegen, interpret, to
Ausrüstung, equipment
Aussage, statement
ausschlaggebend, paramount
ausschliessen, exclude, to
aussehen, appearance
ausserordentlich, extremely
Aussicht, prospect
ausstatten mit, furnish with, to
Ausstattung, equipment
ausstehend *(Rechnungsbetrag)*, outstanding
Ausstellung, exhibition
austauschen, barter, to

Auswahl, selection
ausweiten, extend, to
Auswirkung, effect
automatisieren, automate, to
Automatisierung, automation
bald, shortly
Ballen, bale
Band, tape
Bankier, banker
bar bei Bestellung, cash with order (CWO)
bar bei Lieferung, cash on delivery (COD)
Bargeldautomat, cash dispenser
basieren, base, to
beachten, observe, to
bearbeiten, process, to
bedauern, regret, to
Bedienung, operation
Bedienungsperson, operator
bedingungslos, unconditionally
Bedürfnis, need
beeinflussen, affect, to, influence, to
befördern, convey, to
Beförderung, promotion
begegnen, encounter, to
Beginn, commencement
begleichen, meet, to, settle, to
Begleitbrief, covering letter
begleiten, accompany, to
begrenzen, limit, to
Begünstigter, beneficiary
behandeln, deal with , to, treat, to
Beherrschung, command
beifügen, attach, to, add, to
Beilage, enclosure
beilegen, enclose, to
beinhalten, contain, to, entail, to
Beispiel, instance
beitragen, contribute, to
beiwohnen, attend, to
Bekannte(r), Bekanntschaft, acquaintance
Beleg, reference
beliefern, provide, to
Bemühung, endeavour
Benachrichtigung, notification
bereitstellen, supply, to
Bericht, report
berichtigen, rectify, to
Beschaffenheit, quality
beschaffen, supply,to
Beschluss verabschieden, pass a resolution, to

beschränkt, limited
Beschwerde, complaint
beschädigen, damage, to
Besitz, possession
besonders, particularly
beste Grüsse, kind regards
bestehen, be in existence, to
bestehen auf, insist on, to
Bestellformular, order form
Bestellung, order
Bestellung ausführen, execute an order, to
bestimmte, particular
Bestimmung(sort), destination
bestätigen, cfm (= confirm) / acknowledge, to
Bestätigung, confirmation, acknowledgement
Bestätigung vorbehalten, subject to confirmation
bestürzen, upset, to
betonen, point out, to, emphasize, to
betrachten, regard, to
betrauen mit, entrust with, to
betreffend, concerning, regarding
betreiben, carry out, to, enforce payment, to
Betriebswirtschaft, business administration
Beweis, proof
bewerben, apply, to
Bewerber, applicant
Bewerbung, application
Bezugnahme, reference
Bildschirm, video display unit, (display) screen
Bildschirmgerät, VDU (visual display unit)
Blatt, sheet
blühen, flourish, to
Bonitätsauskunft, status inquiry
Botschaft, message
Branchenverzeichnis, trade index
buchen, enter, to
Buchhaltung, accounting
buchstäblich, literally
Computerausdruck, print-out
Computerkunde, computing science
dankbar, grateful
darlegen, set out, to
darüberhinaus, in addition
Dateiwartung, file maintenance procedure
datieren, date, to

Datenschutz, data protection
dauerhaft, durable
Deckel, lid
definitiv, final
delegieren, delegate, to
Depositenkonto, deposit account
Detaillist, retailer
d.h., i.e.
Diebstahl, theft
direkte Verbindung mit, on-line
Direktion, management
Direktor, manager
Drucker, printer
Druckrad, daisy wheel
Drucksache, printed matter
Effekten, securities
Ehre, honour
eigentlich, actual
Eigentum, property
Eignung, suitability
ein wenig, slightly
einbeulen, dent, to
Einbruch, burglary
einfach, straightforward
einführen, adopt, to
eingeschrieben, registered
Einheit, unit
einlösen, cash, to
einräumen, grant, to
einschreiben, register (a letter), to
Einrichtung, establishment
Einsendung, entry
einsetzen, insert, to
einstellen, employ, to
Einstellung, adjustment
eintönig, dull
einwickeln, wrap, to
Einzelhändler, retailer
Einzelheiten, particulars
eliminieren, eliminate, to
empfehlen, recommend, to
Empfehlung, recommendation
Empfänger, recipient
enorm, huge
enthalten, include, to
entladen, unload, to, discharge, to
entschuldigen, sich, apologize, to
entschädigen, compensate, to
Entschädigung, compensation
entsprechend, accordingly
enttäuschen, disappoint, to
entwerfen, entwickeln, design, to, draft, to, draw up, to
Entwurf, draft

Erbschaft, inheritance
Erfahrung, experience
erfassen, record, to
Erfolgsrechnung, financial statement
ergänzen, replenish, to, supplement, to
erhalten, obtain, to
erhältlich, obtainable
erheblich, considerable
Erkundigung, status inquiry
erleichtern, facilitate, to, simplify, to
erleiden, incur, to
Erlös, proceeds
ermutigen, encourage, to
ermöglichen, enable, to
erreichen, achieve, to
Ersatz, replacement
Ersatzforderung, claim for compensation
Ersatzteile, spare parts
erschaffen, create, to
Ersparnisse, savings
erstaunlich, astonishing
erste, initial
ersuchen, request, to, apply, to
Ertrag, yield
Erwägung, consideration
Erweiterung, extension
erzeugen, create, to
Fabrik, works, factory
Fach, shelf
Fähigkeit, ability, qualification
fällig, due
Fall, case
Fass, barrel
fehlen, lack
Fehlersuche, fault-finding, debugging
(Fernseh)zuschauer, viewer
Fertigprodukt, manufactured good
fest stehend, fixed
feststellen, state, to
Feuerzeug, lighter
Filiale, branch
flau, slack
flexibel, flexible
Flugblatt, leaflet
Flugzeug, aircraft, airplane, aeroplane
flüssig, liquid
Forderung einreichen, file a claim, to
Formgebung, design
Formular, form
Forschung, research
fortsetzen, resume, to
Fracht, freight
Fracht(spesen), carriage

Frachtbrief, bill of lading
Frachtführer, carrier
franko, carriage paid
franko Schiff, fob / free on board
früher, previously
fördern, promote, to
führend, leading
für uns, on our behalf
füttern, feed, to
Gebiet, area, domain, territory
Gebrauch machen von, take advantage of, to
gebrauchen, employ, to
gedruckt, printed
Gedächtnis, memory
geeignet, appropriate
Gefahr, threat, danger
gefesselt, intrigued
gegen bar, on a cash basis
Gegenofferte, counter-offer
gegenseitig, mutual
Gegenvorschlag, counter-proposal
Gehalt, salary
gekreuzter Check, crossed cheque, cheque with restrictive endorsement
Geldverleiher, money-lender
gelegen sein, be convenient, to
gelegentlich, occasionally
genau schildern, detail, to
Genauigkeit, accuracy
geringfügig, minor
Geschwindigkeit, speed
Geschäft abschliessen, settle a deal, to
Geschäfte tätigen, do business, to
Geschäftsabschluss, transaction
Geschäftsbeziehung, business relationship
gesondert, under separate cover
Gestell, rack
gewähren, grant, to
gewährleisten, ensure, to
Gewinn, profit
gewöhnen (an), accustom (to), to
Gläubiger, creditor
gleichartig, similar
GmbH, Inc. (Incorporated)
Goldbarren, gold bar
Grosshandel, wholesale, wholesaling
Grösse, size
Grossist, wholesaler
gründen, establish, to
gründlich, thoroughly
Grundstück, property
Grundstücksmakler, estate agent

gültig, valid
günstig, favourable
günstig abschneiden im Vergleich mit, compare favourably with
Gutachten, survey
Güter, goods
Hafen(anlagen), docks
Haftpflicht, third party liability
Haftung, liability
Halbfabrikate, semi-finished product
Handel, trade
Handelskammer, chamber of commerce
Handelsverkehr, commerce
handhaben, handle, to
Händler, trader
Harass, crate
häufig, frequently
herausgeben, issue, to
herstellen, manufacture, to
Hersteller, manufacturer
herzlich, cordial
Hilfe, assistance
Honorar, fee
hübsch, handsome
ignorieren, ignore, to
im Doppel, in duplicate
im In- und Ausland, at home and abroad
im voraus, in advance
Importabgaben, import duties
in Betracht ziehen, consider, to
in Form von, in the form of
in Frage stehend, in question
in Harasse verpackt, crated
in Pension gehen, retire, to
in Worte fassen, couch, to
in der Einlage, on deposit
in die Irre gehen, go astray, to
inbegriffen, included
Index, index
indossieren, endorse, to
Informatik, computing science, informatics
Inhabercheck, bearer cheque
Inhalt, contents
Inkasso, collection
Inkassobüro, collection agency
inländisch, inland
Inserat, advertisement, ad
Inserent, advertiser
inserieren, advertise, to
Inspektor, surveyor
Inventar, inventory
Inventur machen, take stock, to
Investition, investment

jährlich, annual
Jahrzehnt, decade
Kampagne, campaign
Kapitalzuwachs, capital appreciation
Kapitän, shipmaster
kaufen, purchase, to
Kaufmann, merchant
kaum, hardly
Kenntnis, knowledge
Kenntnis nehmen von, note, to
Kiste, case
knapp, in short supply
Kolonne, column
kompliziert, complicated
Konkurrent, competitor
Konkurrenz, competition, competitors
Konkurrenzfähig, competitive
Konnossement, bill of lading
Konto, account
Kontoauszug, statement of account
Kontokorrent, current account, checking account (US)
Kontoübersicht, S/A, statement of account
Kontrolleur, supervisor
kontrollieren und gegenkontrollieren, cross-checking
Kosten, Versicherung und Fracht, cif / cost, insurance, freight
Kredit, loan
Kreditwürdigkeit, credit rating
Kriegsrisiko, war risk
Kunstseide, artificial silk
Kurs, course
Kündigung, notice
kürzlich, recent(ly)
künftig, prospective
Ladung, cargo
Lager, stock
Lagerist, stockkeeper
Lagerliste, stock records
lagern, store, to
Lagerung, storage
lancieren, launch, to
lästig, inconvenient
Lastwagen, van
Lattenkiste, crate
Laufbahn, career
Lebenslauf, data sheet, curriculum vitae, resumé
lebhaft, brisk
leicht verderbliche Waren, perishables
Lieferant, supplier
liefern, deliver, to

Lieferschein, delivery note
Lieferung, delivery, shipment
Liegestuhl, deck chair
Lösung, solution
Lücke, gap
Luftfracht, air cargo, air freight
Luftfrachtbrief, air waybill
Magaziner, stockkeeper
Mahnbrief, collection letter
Mahnung, reminder
Makler, broker
mangelhaft, faulty
Mängelrüge, complaint
Manko, short shipment
manuell, manual
Marke, brand
Marktforschung, market research
Marktpreis, spot price
Maschinen, equipment
Massengüter, bulk cargo
massgebend, relevant
Meinung, view
Meldung, notice
Memo, message slip
Menge, quantity
Merkmal, feature
Messe, fair
Mietbetrag, rental
Miete, rent
minderwertig, inferior
Missbrauch, misuse
mit Hilfe von, by means of
mit freundlichen Grüssen, yours faithfully
mit freundlichen Grüssen, sincerely yours
mitteilen, inform, to, notify, to
Mitteilung, message, notice
Mitteilungszettel, message slip
mündlich, verbal
Muster, sample, pattern
nachbestellen, reorder, to
Nachbestellung, repeat order
Nachfrage, demand
Nachlässigkeit, negligence
Nähe, vicinity
neuerdings, lately
nicht-haftender Belag, non-stick coating
Norm, requirements
Notierung, quotation
nötigen, compel, to
Notizen, minutes
Notizen machen, take notes, to

Nutzen, benefit
Obligation, bond
obligatorisch, compulsory
ökonomisch, economical
offenbar, evidently
optischer Belegleser, optical reader
ordentlich, neat
örtlich, locally
Paket, parcel, package
Pappe, cardboard
Pappschachtel, carton
passend, suitable
Pauschalabfindung, lump sum
periphere Einheit, peripherals
personalisieren, personalise, to
Pneu, tyre
Police, policy
Post, mail
postwendend, by return (of) mail
Prämie, premium
Preisangabe, quotation
pro Jahr, per annum
Probeauftrag, trial order
Prospekt, leaflet
Protokoll, minutes
provisorisch, provisional
Prozess, lawsuit
Qualität, quality
Quartal, quarter
Quittung, (cash) receipt
Rabatt, discount
Rechenmaschine, calculating machine
Rechnung, account, invoice
Rechnungswesen, accountancy
Recht vorbehalten, reserve the right, to
rechtfertigen, justify, to
rechtlich bindend, legally binding
Rechtsweg beschreiten, take legal action, to
Referent, referee
Referenzen ermitteln, take up references, to
regelmässig, regular
regeln, deal with, to
Register, index
Reiseplan, itinerary
Reparatur, repair
Rendite, yield
Rest, remainder
riesig, vast
robust, durable
roh, hier: Rohöl, crude
Rohmaterial, raw material
rostfrei, stainless

Rückfrage, query
Rückhalt, backing
Rückschlag, setback
Rückstände, arrears
Rückversicherung, reinsurance
rückzahlbar, repayable
Rückzahlung, repayment
Ruf, standing
Saldo, balance
Satz, sentence
Schaden, damage, loss
Schaden melden, file a claim, to
Scheibe (hier: Plattenspeicher), disk
schicklich, proper
Schirm, screen
schnell, speedy
Schnelligkeit, speed
Schreibautomat, word processor
Schritte unternehmen, take steps, to
Schublade, drawer
Schuhwerk, footwear
Schuld begleichen, settle a debt, to
schuld sein, be at fault, to
Schulden, debts, arrears
schulden, owe, to
Schuldner, debtor
Schwankung, fluctuation
schätzen, estimate, to
Schätzung, estimate
schützen vor, protect from, to
selbständig, independent
sich beziehen auf, refer to, to
sich einig werden, come to terms, to
sich leisten, afford, to
sich nähern, approach, to
Sicherheit, security
sichern, secure, to
sicherstellen, ensure, to
sinken, decrease, to
Sichtwechsel, sight draft
Sitzung, meeting
sofort, instantly
sortieren, sort, to
Sortiment, range
sparen, save, to
Spargeld, savings
Sparkonto, savings account
Spediteur, shipper, forwarding agent
Spezialartikel, feature
Spezifikation, specification
Stammkunde, regular customer
stapeln, stack, to
stark gefragt, in heavy demand
steigen, rise, to

Stelle, position, post
Stellung, employment
Steuer, tax
streng, stringent, severe
tabellarisch (an)ordnen, tabulate, to
Tabelle, table
Tagebuch, diary
Tarif, rate
Taschenkalender, diary
Tastatur, keyboard
tatsächlich, actually
Techniker, engineer
Teil, part
teilnehmen, attend, to
Teilzahlung, payment on account
tendieren, tend, to
teuer, expensive
Textverarbeitung, word processing
Thema, topic
Tiefstand erreichen, get low, to
Tochterunternehmen, subsidiary
Traktandum, topic
Transport(kosten), carriage
Transportunternehmer, carrier
Transportversicherung, marine insurance
Treffen, meeting
Treibstoff, fuel
trennen, divide, to
Trommel, drum
typisch, typical
Übereinkunft, agreement
Übereinkunft erlangen, reach an agreement, to
übereinstimmen, tally with, to
überfällig, overdue
übermitteln, convey, to
übernehmen, adopt, to
überprüfen, examine, to
Überprüfung, inspection
überschreiten, be in excess of, to
Überschrift, heading
übersehen, overlook, to
übersteigen, exceed, to
Überwachung, control system
Überweisung, transfer
üblich, usual
Überziehung, overdraft
Umfang, extent
umfassen, cover, to, comprise, to
Umfrage, survey, questionnaire(s)
Umgebung, environment
umgehend, prompt
umkippen, overturn, to

Umriss, outline
umrüsten, retooling
Umsatz, turnover
Umstand, circumstance
Unannehmlichkeit, inconvenience
unbefriedigend, unsatisfactory
unfehlbar, unfailing
unfranko, carriage forward
ungefähr, approximately
ungünstig, unfavourable, adverse
Universalgerät, universal tool
Unkosten, charges
unregelmässig, infrequently
unsererseits, on our part
Unstimmigkeit, discrepancy
unterbreiten, submit, to
Unterkunft, accommodation
unter keinen Umständen, on no account
Unterlage, record
unterlassen, fail, to
Unterlassung, omission
Unternehmen, Unternehmung, company, firm
unterschreiben, sign, to
Unterschrift, signature
Unterstützung, backing
untersuchen, investigate, to
unterwegs, in transit
unwiderruflich, irrevocable
unzulänglich, inadequate
Ursprungsbescheinigung, certificate of origin
Vakanz, vacancy
Verabredung, appointment
verantwortlich, responsible
Verantwortung, responsibility
verarbeiten, process, to
veräussern, dispose of, to
verbessern, perfect, to, improve, to
verbindliches Angebot, firm offer
Verbindung, association
vereinheitlichen, standardize, to
Verfalldatum, due date
verfallen, expire, to
verfertigen, finish, to
Verfügbarkeit, availability
Verhalten, behaviour
verhindern, prevent, to
Verkaufsabrechnung, account sales
verkehrsfähig, negotiable
Verkehrsunfall, motor accident
verlangen, require, to
Verlängerung, extension

verlassen auf, rely on, to
Verleumndung, libel
Verlust, loss
vermindern, reduce, to
Vermögenslage, financial standing
vernünftig, reasonable
Verpackung, package, packing
Verpflichtung *(moralische)*, obligation, commitment
Verpflichtungen nachkommen, begleichen, meet one's liabilities
Verrechnungsstelle, Clearing House
verrichten, perform, to
Versand, consignment
Versandanzeige, advice note
Versandliste, mailing list
Verschiffer, shipper
Versehen, oversight
versehen *(ausstatten)*, provide, to
Versicherer, underwriter, insurer
versichern, insure, to
Versicherung, assurance, insurance
Versicherungsnehmer, policyholder
versprechen, promise, to
Verteiler, distributor
Vertrauen, trust
vertrauenswürdig, trustworthy
vertraulich, confidential, in confidence
vertraut, familiar
Vertreter, representative
Vertretung, agency
verursachen, cause, to
verursacht durch, due to
vervielfältigen, duplicate, to
verwechseln, confuse, to
verweigern, refuse, to
verzögern, delay, to
Vieh, cattle
vielfältig, complex, varied
vierteljährlich, quarterly
vierzehntäglich, fortnightly
von Belang, of consideration
Voranschlag, estimate
Vorausbezahlung, cash with order (CWO)
vorausgesetzt, provided
voraussichtlich, prospective
vorbehältlich, subject to
Vorbereitung, arrangement
vorgängig, beforehand
vorlegen, submit, to
Vorliebe, preference
Vorratsliste, stock records
Vorschlag, proposal

Vorsicht, caution
vorsichtig, cautious
Vorsitzender, chairman
Vorteil, benefit, advantage
vorteilhaft, advantageous, opportune
wägen, weigh, to
Währung, currency
Ware, merchandise, goods
warnen vor, warn of, to
Warnzeichen, warning note
wasserdicht, watertight (cases)
wasserdicht, waterproof (paper)
Weg bahnen, pave the way, to
wegen, due to
weitgehend, extensively
sich wenden an, apply to, to
Werbesendung, commercial
Werbung, advertising, publicity
Wertsachen, valuables
Wertschriften, securities
wesentlich, essential
Wettbewerb, contest
widmen, devote, to
widerstrebend, reluctant
wieder einbringen, recover, to
wieder und immer wieder, over and over again
wiedergewinnen, retrieve, to
Wiederverkauf, resale
Wiederverkäufer, distributor
wirtschaftlich, economical
wirtschafts-, economic
Wissenschafter, scientist
Zahl, figure
zahllos, countless
zahlreich, numerous
Zahlungsbedingungen, terms of payment
Zahlungsempfänger, payee
Zahlungsfähigkeit, solvency
Zeichen, character
zeitraubend, time-consuming
Zentraleinheit, CPU (central processing unit)
zentrieren, centre, to
zerbrechlich, fragile
Zeugnis, testimonial, certificate
ziemlich viel, quite some
Zins, interest
Zoll, customs
Zollabfertigung, customs clearance
Zollerklärung, declaration
zu unseren Gunsten, in our favour
zugeben, acknowledge, to, admit, to

Zugriff, access
zum Beispiel (z.B.), for instance (e.g.)
zurückweisen, reject, to
zur Zeit, currently
zur gegebenen Zeit, in due course
Zusammenfassung, summary
zusammensetzen, compose, to
zusammenstellen, compile, to
Zusatz, addition
zustimmen, approve, to
zusätzlich, in addition, additional
zu unseren Gunsten, on our behalf
zuverlässig, reliable
zuversichtlich, confident
Zweigniederlassung, branch office
Zweck, purpose
zweisprachig, bi-lingual
zwingen, compel, to, oblige, to
Zwischenverkauf vorbehalten, subject
   to goods being unsold
Zwischenzeit, meantime